PRAISE FOR CATHERINE COOKSON

'Humour, toughness, resolution and generosity are Cookson virtues . . . In the specialised world of women's popular fiction, Cookson has created her own territory.'

—Helen Dunmore, *The Times*

'Queen of raw family romances'

—*Telegraph*

'Catherine Cookson soars above her rivals'

—*Mail on Sunday*

'Catherine Cookson is an icon; without her influence, I and many other authors would not have followed in her footsteps.'

—Val Wood

Before I Go

ALSO BY
CATHERINE COOKSON

Fiction

The Kate Hannigan Series

Kate Hannigan
Kate Hannigan's Girl

The Mary Ann Stories

A Grand Man
The Lord and Mary Ann
The Devil and Mary Ann
Love and Mary Ann
Life and Mary Ann
Marriage and Mary Ann
Mary Ann's Angels
Mary Ann and Bill

The Mallen Novels

The Mallen Streak
The Mallen Girl
The Mallen Litter

The Tilly Trotter Trilogy

Tilly Trotter
Tilly Trotter Wed
Tilly Trotter Widowed

The Hamilton Series

Hamilton

Goodbye Hamilton

Harold

The Bailey Chronicles

Bill Bailey

Bill Bailey's Lot

Bill Bailey's Daughter

The Bondage of Love

Other Fiction

Saint Christopher and the Gravedigger

The Fifteen Streets

Colour Blind

Maggie Rowan

Rooney

The Menagerie

Fanny McBride

Slinky Jane

Fenwick Houses

The Garment

The Blind Miller

Hannah Massey

The Unbaited Trap

Katie Mulholland

The Round Tower

The Glass Virgin

The Nice Bloke

The Long Corridor

The Invitation

The Obsession
The Upstart
The Bonny Dawn
The Branded Man
The Desert Crop
The Lady on my Left
The Blind Years
Riley
The Solace of Sin
The Thursday Friend
A House Divided
Rosie of the River
The Silent Lady

Non-Fiction

Our Kate
Let Me Make Myself Plain
Plainer Still
Her Way

Children's Books

Bill and the Mary Ann Shaughnessy
Matty Doolin
Joe and the Gladiator
The Nipper
Our John Willie
Mrs Flannagan's Trumpet
Go Tell it to Mrs Golightly
Lanky Jones
Rory's Fortune

Before I Go

CATHERINE COOKSON

LAKE UNION

PUBLISHING

Published by Lake Union Publishing, Seattle

www.apub.com

Amazon, the Amazon logo, and Lake Union Publishing are trademarks of Amazon.com,
Inc., or its affiliates.

ISBN-13: 9781612184210
ISBN-10: 1612184219

Cover design by Lisa Horton

Printed in the United States of America

We wish to thank all the picture sources, which include The University of Newcastle
upon Tyne, The Howard Gotlieb Archival Research Center, Boston University
and The Catherine Cookson Charitable Trust. While every effort has been made
to trace copyright sources, Amazon Publishers would be grateful to hear from any
unacknowledged copyright holders.

PROLOGUE

AN EXPLANATION OF CATHERINE'S DECLINING HEALTH
AROUND THE TIME OF WRITING

From my unknown father, I inherited something called HHT, hereditary haemorrhagic telangiectasia – a very rare vascular trouble. Its first tangent was anaemia, but we didn't categorise tiredness under that name eighty years ago.

Should I baulk at being sent out on a 'message' or doing another task by saying, 'I'm tired, our Kate' – our Kate was my mother – the answer I was invariably given was, 'Work it off. You'll cope.'

Then one day in 1984, as I was assiduously correcting my work, I found I was reading with my head well to the side and the print wasn't as clear as usual. I put a hand over my left eye. Oh, I could see all right. I put a hand over my right eye. I remember getting to my feet, startled. There was nothing there except a sort of light at the side.

Within a couple of days, I was in hospital and going through tests.

'I'm afraid,' said the specialist, 'you've had it as far as this eye is concerned.' Or words to that effect. It transpired that one of the HHT veins had burst in the back of the eye, and there was nothing that could be done about it.

Anyway, I recall I came out of that hospital very dismayed. Apart from a little peripheral light in my left eye, I had only one eye. The effect was strange, to say the least. I felt for a time that I was only half the person I had been. I was finding that the peripheral light from the dead eye was interfering with the good one. The wearing of an eyeshade was suggested, but I couldn't take to it. I could still see: that was the main thing.

I was writing more than ever now, publishing two books a year and stockpiling others. My brain was a machine that had to be constantly oiled with words.

I may say here that I was only able to work at this pace because of the invaluable assistance given me by my husband in all ways. He nursed me, he cooked, he advised and, if possible, he wouldn't allow anyone but himself to do anything for me. It has always been like that. So he went on unselfishly giving me his life, and I went on working it off and coping.

During this period, constant bleeding was lowering my resistance, so when one day the peripheral light from the left eye seemed to take over and mix the print on the page, it was time to pay yet another visit to my optician.

He was a kind man, my general optician, and did not inform me what was happening, but instead took the course of giving me 'stronger' glasses: four pairs in a short time. Then, one terrifying day, the print on the page was obscured by a light fog. It was as if someone close by had been smoking.

Again the specialist was at my bedside. He was kind but frank.

'You're eighty-four, Mrs Cookson,' he said. 'And I'm afraid you have what age brings: macular degeneration.'

Then his next words nearly caused me to vomit in front of him. 'You won't actually go blind; you'll still be able to make out shapes,' he said.

Oh God, I'm going to be blind. The word blind screamed in my head. I, Catherine Cookson, the writer whose life depended upon her writing – at least her mental stability depended upon her using her brain and the only way she could do that was to write – was going blind. *Oh God!*

The specialist's voice came to me as if from a long tunnel, saying, 'You can get all kinds of magnifying glasses that will help you to read, at least for a time.'

At least for a time.

You won't actually go blind; you'll be able to make out shapes.

'How soon will it come, I mean . . . ?'

He knew what I meant and he said, 'Oh, in some cases, it's a gradual process; in others . . . Well, you can't tell. But don't worry, you'll find ways of coping . . .'

I won't! I won't! Not with this! My lips did not voice the screaming in my head. 'Cope,' he'd said. Cope? I'd been coping all my life. Work it off, Kate had said. You'll cope. I had so far coped with various bodily illnesses, with losing four babies, with going almost mad in a breakdown, and here I had been in bed for the best part of four years owing to continual bouts of bleeding, and I had coped. But no more. No more. This was the finish . . .

Some days later, around two o'clock in the morning, I was sitting up in bed. Tom was still holding one of my hands. He could say no words of comfort, for we had discussed yet again the visit of the young man who had called with four different kinds of magnifying apparatus – from the usual hand ones to one that looked like a television – but the impeding slowness of the appearing words irritated me beyond measure.

I looked to the future. There wasn't any. By this time, I couldn't read a line. I could write, but I couldn't see what I had written; or, worse still, I couldn't remember exactly what I had written.

I had always had a wonderful memory, but this now was seemingly being affected by the loss of my sight.

Work it off. You'll cope.

Not anymore, Kate. Not anymore.

Another saying of hers came to my mind. 'God will provide, lass. God will provide.'

God?

What had God done for me? Hard work and grind all my life, coupled with most of the illnesses my body could take and the mental torments of shame and rejection. He hadn't left anything out, had He? *God will provide?*

He had provided for me all right.

I had never been given to self-pity because I knew there were people a thousand times worse off physically than myself – and mentally too. Whatever had been thrust on me had been countered by my being given the power to cope.

Cope be damned . . . That word! Well, this was one time that I wasn't going to cope. I was a writer who couldn't write; I was a painter who couldn't paint – during the previous few years, under Tom's urging, I had taken up painting again just to give me a break from my daily and incessant routine – so what was there for me to do now? Sit here in this bed waiting for Tom to read the mail to me? To read the headlines? To do the crossword?

No. I wouldn't have this – and it didn't help me when a friend who should have known better said, 'I've no idea how you must feel; I only know if it was me I wouldn't be able to stand it. I'd finish it.'

Not having listened to radio programmes for such a long time, one night I switched the radio on haphazardly and heard some men talking. To my astonishment, it dawned on me that they were blind. Each described his reactions to approaching blindness. The effect on me, forgive the pun, was very enlightening. No longer did I feel absolutely isolated. These men were talking, and telling each other, of their own particular agony.

I switched off and asked Tom to look up the title of the programme. It was *In Touch*. And a comforting phrase came into my mind regarding these men: the camaraderie of the blind.

From this time, it seemed that a light did appear at the end of the tunnel. I had become increasingly distressed about the sorting out of my food on the plate, no matter how Tom might have arranged it, and the feel of a messy table napkin could almost bring me to tears. Also, I was forever picking up small, non-existent black objects from the sheet or the bed cover.

Thankfully, through listening to *In Touch*, I was assured that this was just one of the phobias of approaching blindness.

Whereas for months my mind had been dwelling on an easy way out, I now returned to my 'inner voice' that had always guided me. Call it soul or subconscious or spirit – whatever – it had, in times of great need, given me answers to my despairing questions; answers which, at the time, did not seem to apply to my present need, but which turned out to be right in the end. And this time, to my plea, it said, 'Go on putting your stories down on tape.' And I cried back at it, 'What's the good? I can't correct them.' To which came the answer, 'Tom can read them to you and you can dictate the alterations to him. And just as you used to delete and scribble alterations between the lines, he can do the same.'

So it came to pass that I ordered my days. Beginning with the mail, Tom would read a letter to me, and I would dictate my reply to him. This generally took the whole morning if there were no interruptions. After lunch, we would carry on in the same way with the typescript of a story.

During any break, I would return to the tape and continue to dictate my tale.

The last thing we did at night was the *Telegraph* crossword.

Of course, nothing runs this smoothly: often the HHT interfered; at times, too, we both felt exhausted and could not go on – Tom at eighty and I at eighty-six.

The main thing was that I was indeed working it off and coping again. And I say with assurance that I could now look ahead to the time I had left knowing that I could continue to provide some measure of happiness or entertainment for my readers, while I myself was being stimulated by what I heard each week listening to *In Touch*.

◆ ◆ ◆

Here I am on an island waiting to start a new life as the days gallop towards death – for the days of age are not only much shorter than those in youth, but they rush away from you at a frightening rate.

Take a day: a day in youth is an experience, and the last hour is as far away as a child's Christmas; a day in age is but a dim memory in a week that is already gone.

At least, so time is for me. Yet I savour it more as it rushes from me, leaving a chilly blush; but when I lose the savour, I will know the gallop is nearing its end and then all time will be mine – the sixtieth second will have enveloped eternity.

But before I go, I'd like to relate some events from my life. Not as stated, but as it really was: filled with illness, doctors, dogs, jealousy and evil from which I emerged only because of the love of an exceptional man.

1

Catherine Cookson was born Catherine (Katie) Ann McMullen by Tyne Dock in South Shields (near Newcastle) in 1906, one of the poorest areas in Britain at the time. She was raised by her grandparents, Rose and John McMullen, and grew up believing that her mother, Kate Fawcett, who was not married, was her sister. The stigma that illegitimacy carried with it at this time had a great and long-lasting effect on Catherine – not least the hereditary vascular disease, haemorrhagic telangiectasia, she suffered from and that remained undiagnosed for many years – as did her mother's alcoholism.

At the age of thirteen, Catherine left school, undertaking a variety of work before getting a job at the laundry at Harton Workhouse in South Shields. In 1929, at the age of twenty-three, she moved South to work as a laundress in a workhouse near Clacton in Essex. The following year, she settled in Hastings. This seaside town was where she bought her first house, where she met and married her husband, Tom, and began to write.

In 1976, Catherine and Tom moved back to the North-East.

Sunday, 19 February 1984

I had promised myself that I wasn't going to do another thing on this tape recorder for at least a year. Only a fortnight ago, I finished *Harold*, which made it nine books awaiting publication. Doubting very much if I'd see many of them published, I thought I should take Tom's advice and call it a day at last.

On Friday, five days after making this decision, and with one of my numerous complaints playing up, I decided to stay in bed. This didn't mean rest, for I seemed to get more work done both on the tape and in correcting when I had my legs up. So when, by that morning's post, I received from my secretary, Sarah, seventy-odd pages of the rough of *Harold* that she had taken down from the tapes, I thought, 'Good, I'll get through those today.'

The checking of that rough script took me from eight in the morning till five in the afternoon with only half an hour break in between, and as I came to the last page, feeling very tired, I realised that I was holding my head on one side. I also became aware that I'd been doing this a lot of late . . . Why? To find out, I put my hand over my right eye, looked down on the page with my left and for a moment couldn't take in the fact that I could see only a black blur. I was unable to read one word.

My eyes have always troubled me more or less, and five years ago I saw a specialist because of the constant pain over my left eye. He reported that the trouble could be one of five things, but he didn't know which one. Why, I asked myself now, hadn't he tried to find out? When, two years ago, my eyes were still troubling me, I changed my optician. This man said, 'Oh, your eyes are perfectly healthy, marvellous for your age.' I was then seventy-five. But when my healthy eyes began to give me more and more trouble – the trouble being constant pain, which I tried to rectify with reading in stronger lights – I went back to my optician. The first thing I said to him was, 'Do you think I should see a specialist?' No, no, he said, he couldn't see any need at present. There was something at the back of the left eye, but people of my age usually got this kind of thing. Because of 'this kind of thing', I became carsick at night, owing to the flashing lights which I was seeing double and treble of, especially the red ones.

Now I came to the Friday night when I realised I had only one sighted eye and that was painful too. I don't think I panicked. No, I didn't. In the back of my mind I'd been expecting this for a long time. In fact, all my life it had been one of my main fears, healthwise, that I should lose my sight. There are no truer words than, 'The thing that is feared comes upon you.'

At this point, my main reaction was anger. My trouble in that eye hadn't started today or yesterday – it had been there a long time. It should have been seen to: I remembered complaining about this eye twenty years ago in Hastings.

It happened that the phone was off for three days and I couldn't contact my first optician until Monday morning, during which time I'd done a lot of thinking. What was there about me that I was being called upon to face another fight? Hadn't I had enough? And what was there about me that seemed to be in touch with something outside myself – or more correctly, deep within myself? For, three weeks ago, hadn't I had my naked dream?

For years now, I've only had to dream that I see myself naked for something in the way of illness to hit me. If I'm only naked to the waist, well, as I've proved over the years, that bare torso heralds bouts above the belt: three incidents of pneumonia followed three such dreams. Once, I dreamed I looked in the mirror and saw my bare back. Some days later (at last, I may say) I was given an X-ray, the results of which elicited the remark from my then doctor, 'It's horrific.' Apparently, there was arthritis on both sides of the spine, the bottom vertebra was locked and twisted and, to use his own words, the rest was mush. He didn't know how I'd walked for years. His previous comments had been, 'Ninety-nine people out of a hundred have backache, so what?'

Another bare torso proved to be a hiatus hernia. Two bare legs didn't prophesy that I was going to lose them, just that I had contracted phlebitis. However, I cannot remember being given any warning of an allergy to practically all kinds of food. And, of course, I was born with telangiectasia, kindly passed on to me from my unknown father.

So when a month ago, I saw myself completely starkers, I thought, '*Oh no, no, no*. Not again.' I was so disturbed that I woke Tom in the middle of the night, saying 'I've had my bare dream again.' It's a wonder he didn't say, 'Pull the clothes around you then.' In his place, I would have.

What he said was, 'Now, you made up your mind that you weren't going to take any notice of it, didn't you?'

'Yes,' I said. 'But it was very vivid. It . . . it somehow indicated that whatever's going to happen is going to alter my whole life. Something will affect my whole body.'

Poor man, the things he's had to put up with. Two days following, I got a little snifter of a cold. I thought, here we go again. If I have pneumonia now, that'll finish me. Well, something's got to do it in the end. But no, it was only a little snifter.

Tom said, 'You should wear woollens.'

I said, 'When I wear woollens, I'm always getting colds.'

Anyway, days passed, I waited for something to hit me, but nothing did. It was wonderful. That was that: the end of superstition, premonition, the lot. Until that Friday night.

By the Monday morning, I fully realised what my naked dream was telling me. Sight guided the body; my whole life would indeed be affected from now on.

As soon as my optician looked into the left eye, he said immediately, 'You must go to the hospital to see a specialist.'

I got in touch with David Harle, my doctor. When I described what had happened, he gave me a further shock by saying, 'That's bad.' But he speeded things up and by three o'clock I was in the hospital, where the verdict was that damage had been done to the eye and not just recently. It would appear that a telangiectases [spider] vein had broken at the back of the eye.

The following day, I was in the hospital again, and was told that nothing could be done for the left eye. When I asked the specialist if the deterioration in the right eye could be arrested by laser beams, he gave it to me straight: No, he couldn't guarantee that anything would deter the deterioration of the right eye. Of course, it was my age too – seventy-seven. This man felt he could be blunt.

Well, I didn't feel seventy-seven and I didn't act or look seventy-seven, but my body wasn't listening to me.

Tom had been with me during these two visits, and when we came out he said, 'It's like a curse upon you. People always give it to you straight from the shoulder. They think you're tough.'

On the way home, he tried to drive the car with one hand while he held mine with the other, until I said, 'Look, whatever way I have to go, or we have to go, I don't want it to be in a car accident. It's too messy.'

But it is strange that all my life people have treated me as if I can take it on the chin. Again and again, it's been said to me, 'You're a fighter; you'll come through.' Even David said, 'I don't worry about you. You'll beat it.'

I'm not tough. I'm a weepy, frightened individual inside. Having said that, I know there is something inside me, or someone on the outside working for me, that usually helps me through. Perhaps it's the Spiritual Healers[1]. That was the first thing I did when the phone came on again on Monday morning: I rang Ray Branch at The Sanctuary, and he, dear man, said, 'We are all rooting for you, every one of us.'

I've been thinking that perhaps I have the final lesson to learn and this is the only way it will come about. If I believe there's a power – give it what name you like, God, or anything else – then I've got to openly acclaim that power, but not through any denomination, oh no. Yet, there is always the feeling in me that I want to go into a church, because I come nearer to something there, but I tell myself that this is only the overflow from those early days in Tyne Dock when I could never pass the church without being fascinated by its garish ornamentation in the daylight and the attraction of the sanctuary lamp in the dark.

---

1   The Harry Edwards Spiritual Healing Sanctuary in Surrey.

In the changed sight that lies before me, perhaps I will find the answer to the great unease within me; the reason why success means very little, and why the love and appreciation of my work poured out in the letters that I receive daily hardly touches me – though I do feel compelled to answer any cries for help.

Here lies a paradox again: two thirds of every letter I receive tells me of the strength that the reader perceives in me and how it has helped them to carry on. This is a mystery to me. I suppose it's the simple fact that I cannot see myself as others see me: I feel that I'm still Katie McMullen from East Jarrow, not the famous Catherine Cookson, as I'm supposedly known. I feel I am a very ordinary individual.

Yet there is another contradiction here: in the quietude of the night, I recognise a being in me that gives me the answer to many things, that guides me, that tells me that my life has a purpose, and that by just being myself I am fulfilling it. But that is in the night. In the light of day, I see this woman who is impatient, critical and, as Tom says, 'A time and motion wallah . . .' But it's marvellous that he and I think mostly alike. We see people from the same standpoint; our judgements are the same on most things – especially on morality. So much so that after reading a newspaper or looking at the television, at times we seem to be two of a species on another planet.

Well now, I'd better come to the point. Being unable to read much, I'll just have to talk, and as memories come flooding back from those far-off days of my childhood and my youth and middle age, I'll jot them down as they come to mind, remembering that I've said a great deal in my first autobiography, which ended when I was fifty. A great deal has happened in the last twenty-seven years yet, on looking back, not as much happened as happened before and which I left out of *Our Kate*.

◆ ◆ ◆

Back to February, 1984

It's been a traumatic fortnight, where sympathy about my plight has infuriated me at times instead of soothing me.

'Oh, Kitty, you'll stand up to this; you'll face it like you've done everything else. It's just another mountain for you to climb.'

On and on. Even if they had witnessed me crying on Tom's shoulder, I don't think they would have changed their opinion about my toughness.

But I had to smile, if ruefully, when a sympathetic letter from a friend ended by saying, 'Anyway, dear, at your age, you've been left with a nice pair of legs.' Not quite a bon mot – not quite anything.

David, my doctor, burst the bubble when he said, 'Oh, being you, you'll take it in your stride.'

By this time, I'd had enough and I yelled at him, 'I bloody well won't – I'm sick of taking things in my stride.'

'You bloody well will,' he said. And then some.

We were sitting in the conservatory drinking our coffee. Tom came in, then got out as quickly as he could. He said after, 'That was something, you and he at each other.'

2

At the beginning of 1930, Catherine moved from Essex to take up the position of laundress at the Hastings Workhouse². While working there, she became close friends with an Irish woman named Annie (Nan) Smith. They lived together for a period, along with Catherine's mother, Kate – but it was a highly volatile situation, exacerbated by Kate's drinking.

Always a diligent saver, by 1933 Catherine had enough put by to buy her first house, a fifteen-roomed Victorian 'gentleman's residence' called The Hurst. She moved in with Nan and Kate – though later both would move out – and took in lodgers and people in need of care to supplement her income, though she stayed on working at the laundry until 1939. One of her lodgers was Tom Cookson, a teacher at Hastings Grammar School, and in June 1940 they married.

Doctors have played an enormous part in my life, from when I was a child to this very day. My first encounter with a doctor may have proved very embarrassing for our Kate, as I said in my autobiography. Discovering that I hadn't got a father, my coming into the world being

---

2   Hastings Workhouse changed its name to Hastings Municipal Hospital in 1930 – around the time Catherine started work there. To avoid confusion, Hastings Workhouse, when not using its full name, is referred to as the Institution throughout.

in the nature of a second Virgin Birth, I made it my business to choose one, and who better than our dear Dr McHaffie? When he kindly gave me a lift to school in his car and I proclaimed to all my school mates that there went my da, I may, inadvertently, have put his whole career at stake. But, thankfully, it didn't turn out like that. He was the same man who told Kate, when she reluctantly took me to see him, that I had to give up pen painting. I was nearly eighteen, and had been earning my living through painting for the past two years, making four shillings profit out of the ten shillings charged for a commission, which completing took up to fifty-five hours. It turned out that my constant feeling of illness was being caused by lead poisoning.

The next doctor I came in contact with was Dr Shanley, who was a medical officer at Harton Workhouse, South Shields. Accompanied by a stiff-faced matron, a sister and a nurse, he entered the isolation room where I'd been hurriedly bundled after two of my contemporaries had noticed I had a number of spots on my tummy. Some of the staff – I was one of them – were being given a free treatment with a violet ray machine, which we had helped the hospital raise funds for, and I had been sitting in my briefs – knickers and brassiere – when my associates remarked on my spots. Within an hour, there I was, in isolation and absolutely bemused until Dr Shanley, after his examination, started to playfully count my spots. On leaving the room followed by the staff, he said, in an aside, 'She's never been touched.' My kind friends of the lamp had, I realised, hoped that they had spotted syphilis.

It is a saying that one should forgive and forget; that saying is rarely quoted by anyone who has suffered at the hands of their enemies – which include workmates or indeed friends. The wounds they inflict rankle. At that time, my one desire was to be a lady and a writer – I don't know which I put first. Anyway, the overriding feeling of my life was to be respectable. I hadn't a name to call my own except the one that had been pinned on me by being brought up by my step-grandfather, John McMullen, and which I held, you could say, almost sacred. To this very day, I like that name and am proud of it. On my wedding day, I thankfully changed it for Cookson, but I am still, underneath the skin, Katie McMullen, that girl who struggled to raise herself above the melee because she knew she was different.

But back to the doctors. When I left Harton in 1929, I went to Manningtree in Essex as a laundress of the Institution. Those were the beginning of my lonely days because that place was stuck out in the wilds, miles from Clacton. And it was on a Saturday afternoon in Clacton that I experienced the heaviest bleeding I'd yet had. I'd started this odd type of bleeding from my nose five years before: I was sitting on the beach when I seemed to have a minor explosion in my head and the blood poured down both my nostrils.

I recall running along a street to a chemist, who, taking a great wad of cotton wool from a roll and putting it across my face, told me to make for a doctor whose surgery was at the end of the street. It was a long street, and before I reached the end of it, I had another weird sensation in my head that caused me to stop. And there down my nose came what looked like an actual vein filled with blood. As I recall, it was about a foot long, and as I leaned against the wall and looked down on it, I knew the bleeding had stopped. The doctor's house was quite near, but I didn't go in because I'd have to pay perhaps three or five shillings, and I wasn't going to do that now the bleeding had stopped. I was saving hard – I'd always saved hard. From ha'pennies to shillings (pounds were more difficult to come by, but twenty shillings made one).

Back in Manningtree at the Institution, the visiting doctor saw me on the Monday morning. His verdict? 'Oh, these things happen.' It was all in the cause of maturing. And I was a young woman, wasn't I?

◆　◆　◆

I left that Institution at the end of January 1930, and took up the position of laundress in the Hastings Workhouse, although I lived out.

It was my second year there when there was a flu epidemic and the assistant matron went down with it. Having myself been taken under the wing of the matron, she asked me to take on this duty while still supervising the laundry. I took up temporary quarters near the porter's lodge, and it was during the second week of this extra duty that I had another big burst. I was used to minor bleedings, which I either managed to stop or let run until they stopped themselves. But this was something like the Clacton one, and when the doctor was called down from the Institution's hospital to see me – it was a separate part – who should it be but my dear Dr Shanley from Harton Workhouse in South Shields. We chatted amicably, and he ordered complete rest with as little movement as possible. But his treatment didn't work, for two days later I was bleeding like a stuck pig, and they rushed me up into the theatre, where I experienced my first cauterisation. That was after they had sent posthaste across town to the East Sussex Hospital for an electric instrument with which to do the cauterising. It was a new thing, I understood.

When the instrument arrived, Mrs Shanley, who was assisting her husband, asked if I'd like to be blindfolded. I can remember replying, 'No, do what you like – you can take my nose off if only you can stop the bleeding.' I remember seeing this 'poker' coming towards me with sparks flying off it, then there was the smell of burning hair as it went up my nose. When it hit the flesh, I nearly hit the ceiling – and would have done if I hadn't been held down.

Cauterisation without real anaesthetic must be experienced before it can evoke sympathy. The memory of that cauterisation made me sit out bleeding rather than calling in the doctor for a long time after.

From my early childhood days, I had been aware of a tiredness in me, but northern people didn't get tired. If they complained about being tired, they were lazy bitches. Everybody, for that matter, could say they were tired: life was hard; you just had to get on with it. But, following the bleedings, I would be assailed by this tiredness and a sort of ill-feeling, as I put it to myself.

Living out, I had to register with a different medical man. His name was Dr Walker. He lived quite near to where I was lodging at the top of Mount Road, Hastings. When, on my first visit, I tried to explain to him how I felt, he gave me a bottle of red stuff and a certificate, which read 'Nervous Debility'.

What was that? I wasn't nervous. I couldn't be nervous in the job I was doing: controlling eleven paid staff and anything between twenty and thirty mentally defective inmates, besides the daily rag-taggle and bobtail that came into the Institution as casuals and had to do a day's work in the laundry to pay for their night's doss and a meal of sorts. You couldn't be nervous having to face that lot, and me the youngest of them all. What did he mean, nervous debility?

When I said, 'I'm bleeding frequently from my nose and my tongue,' his remark was, 'Oh, that'll clear your head . . .' Shades of great-grandmama and ladies in decline.

I was to speak my mind to many doctors after this, but Dr Walker was the first one I rounded on. I had a flat by this time in the centre of the town, two miles away or more from the Institution, and I was also having tummy trouble.

I understood that my dear Dr McHaffie had had to give me treatment when I was born because my bowels wouldn't work. And our Kate and me grannie subjected me to their own treatment for constipation during my young days by inserting a tube of blue mottle soup into the rectum and sitting me on a chamber pot of boiling water . . . Some of the old remedies are marvellous, aren't they, and so ineffective.

So, here I was again, having trouble in the same quarter, only I was suffering bad pain. My doctor was called in, and without any preamble he examined me in much the same way as I've seen a vet examine a horse on a farm. That particular horse neighed loudly; I screamed and, turning on him, I yelled, 'You're a cruel individual.' I should have said bugger, but I didn't swear at that time – that was to come later. As I said, he was the first doctor I rounded on, but I've never stopped since.

I remember he took my railing quite calmly, saying, ''Tisn't me that's cruel, it's the fissure you've got.'

What was a fissure? I learned it was a split in the rectum. Anyway, I swore that that man would never get near me again – at least at my special parts. But I continued to go to him, and I always got the same note: 'Nervous Debility'.

It was when I took The Hurst – my first house – that I became so tired I could hardly get about. But I had to keep my job going, for I had to pay the rent on this 'gentleman's residence'. Whereas before, living in the centre of Hastings, I would take a bus, now I had a two-mile trek across fields morning and evening before starting the day's work helping to put the place to rights. So, once again, Dr Walker visited me.

I had been bleeding badly for a long time . . . but of course, as he said, it would clear my head, and he also informed me that I was of a nervous disposition. I wouldn't believe that. Miss McMullen, running a laundry and a guest house at the same time, of a nervous disposition? *Nonsense.*

What I needed was a tonic, he said. So he gave me a prescription. I was out of bed when I started on the tonic; two days later I was flat on my back. Again, he was looking down on me and sighing, but he was kind this time.

'You must never take tonics in future,' he said. 'Or anything that has strychnine, arsenic or mercury in it, because these ingredients will poison you. In fact, you must always be careful what you have in your medicines.'

That was good to know. I was now prepared against poisoning, but what about the constant bleeding? Well, some people were unfortunate, he said, but I'd better see a specialist.

I was given a note to go to the East Sussex Hospital, where I saw a doctor who was surrounded by students. After the examination, he said, 'Do you pick your nose?'

'No,' I pronounced with deep indignation.

'This patient is suffering from epistaxis,' he informed the students. So that's what I had. I'd been wondering for years. I couldn't wait till I got home and looked at the dictionary. There it was: 'Epistaxis', meaning bleeding of the nose.

◆ ◆ ◆

My personal life was a shambles at this time. My mother was with me and drinking heavily. My so-called friend, Annie Smith, was making my life hell because I had fallen in love with a young schoolmaster called Tom Cookson. Then my mother returned to the North and I set up Nan Smith in a house of her own by mortgaging mine. And in August 1939, I left the laundry in order to look after my house and the epileptic and mentally defective patients I had lodging with me then, together with Captain David Evans and Tom. Captain was a charming con man and he wasn't above stealing from other people in the house, but he forgot his regimental silver napkin ring – I've still got it.

The war broke out, but what did that really matter compared to all the troubles that were on my shoulders? Tom and I wanted to marry, but I was afraid that if we did, I would find him up the alley with his throat slit. And I'm not joking. Nan Smith was eleven years older than me and she had inveigled herself into my life. I had looked upon her as a mother when we first met because she had a husband and a child of her own back in Ireland. She had all the Irish charm and was so very kind to me in the beginning.

I had never really known a mother's love, as Tom has made me aware. Kate didn't come onto my horizon until I was almost six years old. That was the day she came crying into the New Buildings after finding out that her mother and stepfather had moved from the house in Leam Lane – where I was born – without letting her know. The next time I saw her was almost two years later, when she was the worse for drink, coming down Hudson Street in Tyne Dock. But even then, she still wasn't my mother. It wasn't until the children in the back lane told me that the man I called da and the woman I called ma were not my mother and father but my grandma and granda, that I asked myself, 'Then who is our Kate?' She couldn't possibly be my mother 'cos she hadn't got a husband. Anyway, I didn't want her as a mother because she drank.

I must have been around eight years old when she finally came back home to look after her mother and the rest of the household and, of course, she would have been forced to come back because of me. But from the go, I can see that she used me. She used me for borrowing from the neighbours, for going to the pawn shop, for running for the beer, for going on messages, for helping to clean the house, for carrying those big baskets of washing to Jarrow, for picking cinders – and all the while ignoring the tiredness that I continually went on about.

There were lots of things I purposefully left out of my autobiography about Kate – *Our Kate*[3] – because I wanted to put her over as I knew she could have been if she hadn't drunk. So when this woman, Nan Smith, gave me cakes and presents out of her small wage and would run from here to hell for me, she seemed like the mother figure that I had never previously enjoyed. At first, I loved her for it, though this feeling was tested when I discovered she was ripping me off in so many ways. Nan, as I have explained elsewhere, was the means of bringing my mother from the North to live with us and so began my purgatory all over again.

Later, when Nan became my housekeeper in the guest house, I was never out of debt. Yet, at times I had six guests and I myself was earning three pounds and six shillings a week – a big wage in those days. But Nan smoked like a chimney, and she also had a sideline that I didn't know much about then – it must have run in the family because her sister ruined herself with gambling. Nan's weakness was the dogs, and

---

3   Published in 1969.

also dishing out presents to all and sundry, using money filched from the housekeeping.

She liked to be thought of as Diamond Lil, good old Nan, kind old Nan, jolly old Nan. No one saw her as terrible old Nan, old Nan the tyrant. This came to the fore when I met Thomas Henry Cookson, the young schoolmaster who had come to teach mathematics at the Hastings Grammar School. He was lodging with my mother – who was still in Hastings – and he caused Nan to split her sides in private as he followed me around. To her, he was a young lad of twenty-four and I was a woman of thirty. But her laughter turned to rage when she discovered that I was interested in this young lad. She had never acted like this about the other men that had come into my life. In fact, she was quite agreeable to the idea that if a certain man could get a divorce I would marry him – putting aside the fact that I never would. Looking back, I think she counted on this.

The climax came one night when I had got ready to go to a dance at the Institution. The matron had asked me to bring Captain Evans and Tom. I was all ready when Nan gave me an ultimatum: if I went out of that door with Tom, then when we came back we would find her hanging. A terrible row ensued, the result of which was that I asked the men to go on and tell the matron I wasn't well.

Nan had what is called a 'ninth nerve tic' in her face, and every night when I came home from work, there she'd be in the kitchen, holding herself in agony. I didn't find out for a long time that the agony started five minutes before I entered the door. Nan gave me another ultimatum: either I stopped going out with Tom, or she would go to London and have an operation on the nerve – which in ninety cases out of a hundred proved fatal or left one paralysed. It was up to me. Previously, when I had occasionally gone out with Tom to the pictures, we were timed. How long it would take us to get into Hastings, the length of the show – everything was checked and, should my return not coincide with Nan's timing, hell was let loose.

Why did I stand all this?

Firstly, because I relied on Nan to see to the patients, and secondly, because of a failing of mine – an overabundance of gratitude for any kindness shown to me. I have never forgotten any kindness done to me, and I've always tried to repay it, not twofold but tenfold. And I remembered how kind she had been to me in my first years in Hastings when I was lonely and fighting against physical weakness: the constant bleeding and increasing inability to digest food without experiencing excruciating pain at the top of my chest – I hadn't heard of a hiatus hernia at this point.

Even when we were separated and I bought the house for her at the bottom of the road, she still remained a threat. What I didn't know then was that, between Nan and my mother, my name in the town was mud. Hadn't my mother bought me The Hurst and hadn't I turned her out? Hadn't Nan Smith given me years of her life and hadn't I turned her out . . . ?

I'd only given up my job in the Institution for a month when the war started and I was given the choice of filling the house with children or blind people. What with having two mental patients, I couldn't take the children, so I took the blind.

I'd always been sorry for the blind, but on that Sunday night, when the crowded bus disgorged twelve blind men from the East End of London, most of them in sandals and so dirty – and this wasn't the result of bombing, for it hadn't started yet – I was appalled. Some of the men hadn't any underclothing, and those that had were mostly filthy. I often wondered how they had been allowed to live like that.

Out of that twelve, there were about four that were decently dressed. Oh, and of course there was the wife of one of them – the little bossy cockney who saw to it that her and her husband's plates were full by nicking pieces from the others.

I was paid a pound per head per week, out of which I had to feed them, help clothe them, provide ordinary medicines and do their washing. I did the latter by using my feet in the bath and tramping them, as some of their clothing was too filthy to handle – oddly enough, for the fifteen years I had been in the laundry business, I had never actually done any washing. I also provided a 'Tuesday Night at Eight' – named after a programme on the wireless called *Monday Night at Seven* – for them. They had a sing-song, Tom and the old girl and myself and friends danced some of them round, and I provided a few bottles of beer. All out of a pound a week.

I may also mention that I did the cooking. Nevertheless, it was heaven compared to my previous life. I hadn't to get up at seven o'clock in the morning and tramp across those fields in all weathers. There were no harassments or pettiness, or personal, jealous squabbles. This had been the pattern at the Institution starting from the head downward, and all because, it had turned out, the matron, like Nan Smith, wanted to rule my life. Though to give her her due, she liked Tom and wanted us to marry.

At this time, Nan Smith was a sergeant major in the army and because of the debt she had got into, I was managing the business side of her affairs. Her house was also full of blind people and I was trying to keep that afloat too, as it was linked with my own home.

Then came my wedding day, Saturday, 1 June 1940. On the previous Monday, I had received a letter from Nan to say that an officer friend of hers wasn't very well and she had a week's leave and would like to come and spend it at my place. I knew what that meant: everything that happened would be reported back to Nan. So that morning, I had run after Tom as he was going to school and called, 'We'll be married on Saturday.'

During the week that followed, there was an argument with the priest because Tom wasn't a Catholic, and I had told him that if he didn't marry us in church, we would go to a registry office.

In the end, it was arranged that we would be married in church. It was around twelve o'clock on Saturday when I was getting ready that the phone rang. It was Nan. She was bringing a lot of ammunition through from Dover so was down at the other house and she wanted to see me. I had previously written and told her I was going to be married that day. I recall I felt faint. What should I do? If I didn't go down, she would come up. I said to a very nice girl I had helping me at that time, 'I've got to go down to Mrs Smith's. Tell Mr Cookson when he comes in from school I hope I won't be long.'

Tom said that he nearly fainted when he got that message for he never expected to see me again. Anyway, there I was, standing in the kitchen of Elphinstone Mount – Nan's house – and there she was with three other sergeants all jolly and laughing – she the loudest of all. When I said, 'I must get back,' she came out with me into the road and stood at the back of this lorry that was full of rifles and ammunition. They seemed to have been thrown in haphazardly – and likely they had because it was the height of the Dunkirk evacuation, and I understood they had come straight from Dover and were being taken further inland.

I watched her hand play on the butt of one of the rifles. I stared dumbly at her and she at me, then I said, 'Goodbye, Nan.'

She didn't say anything, but as I walked away I knew she had her eyes riveted on me. I crossed the road and went up the broad lane opposite with my legs shaking beneath me. Any minute, I felt I would hear a crack and that would be it, but I didn't hurry. I made myself walk slowly. The road curved sharply, and when I found myself round the bend, I bent over a garden railing and retched. I wasn't dead; she hadn't shot me.

When I eventually reached the house, Tom was as white as a sheet. We fell into each other's arms, but didn't speak.

At two o'clock, I was married. She was out of my life and she would never come back.

What was I talking about? I was a simpleton who as yet knew nothing about jealousy and hate and the guises they could hide under.

3

Though Catherine and Tom were, by all accounts, devoted to each other, the early years of their marriage were shadowed by war. Tom spent five years in the RAF during this time, and Catherine miscarried four pregnancies, a traumatic ordeal which took a toll on both her physical and mental health. In 1945, she suffered a breakdown, and it would take her almost twenty years to recover.

To return to doctors.

Babies had never been discussed in our household. I had come into it as a sin and a shame, so the subject was taboo. But in my early teens, I thought a lot about babies and how they would be made while knowing it was a sin. Being a firm Catholic in those days and sticking to the rule, confession for me meant spilling the beans, because we all knew that we could sin by thought as much as by deed. So there was a period in the confessional when the time was taken up by pouring out my thoughts about babies and things. I should imagine Father O'Keefe looked forward to my coming, because when I inadvertently mentioned the spilling of beans in confession with another Catholic girl, she thought I was potty. But of course, in my naivety I was talking to God, and the priest hadn't the slightest notion who was on the other side of the grid. I realise now that there was a strange innocence about me, and even when I thought I knew everything, that innocence remained. There it was during the first weeks of my marriage to Tom, which were beautiful in spite of me bleeding like a pig every other day and feeling ill most of the time.

We were married only a month when the order came that the school had to be evacuated to St Albans – the whole country was being reshuffled. I received a very strong request to take the twelve blind men with me, also the two mental defectives. I refused with as much politeness as I could gather to cover my utter amazement at such an idea.

So Tom and I landed in St Albans and were billeted with a very nice couple. But I'd had my own house for years and didn't take to sharing with someone else, although they couldn't have been kinder. Fortunately, we found this little flat next to a barber's shop and above an empty shop run as an office for dispatch riders in the main street. The police station was right opposite the flat, the library was on one side of it, the doctor's house on the other, and I'm not sure if the Salvation Army was on that side too. I had brought the best pieces from The Hurst in Hastings, and made a lovely home in the three rooms. We were delightfully happy, even while I seemed to feel worse every day – strangely ill, in fact.

The barber's wife told me of a lady doctor, so I went to see her.

'How long have you been married?' she said.

'Over two months.'

'When was your last period?'

'About two months ago – they're very irregular.'

'You're pregnant.'

'*What!* I'm not.'

'You said you were married, didn't you?'

'Yes.'

'Are you happily married?'

'Yes.' Oh, yes.

'Therefore you sleep with your husband . . . ?'

'Yes, of course.'

'Then you're pregnant.'

I walked out.

Pregnant? I wasn't pregnant. Ridiculous.

Why, I ask myself now, should I have thought it ridiculous? Tom was a very, very normal individual, and so was I. I still can't give myself the answer.

I said to Tom, 'I'm going to see another doctor.'

This time, I had to call a doctor in as I felt too ill to go out. And there he came, a charming man well into his seventies who had been a naval doctor up till he retired, but now, in the emergency, he had been dragged from his hammock and pushed on deck again.

'What's the trouble, my dear?' he said, holding my hand and patting it.

'They say I'm pregnant. I know I'm not.'

'Oh. Well, well, we'll see, won't we?'

He did a little poking around and then said, 'You're right, you're not. Your trouble is you have a stopped bowel.'

I knew it. I knew it.

'But I'll soon put that right. I have some special stuff that I got over from France before the fall. It'll clear your passages.'

The following day, he arrived with the stuff he had got from France before the fall. I had to take a dose night and morning. I did so for a week and nothing untoward happened.

Again, he was sitting by my side, patting my hand and talking now about cosmetics – he had noticed a number of jars on the dressing table. He seemed to know a lot about cosmetics. The foundation of most of them, he said, was lanoline, but that was almost non-existent when it reached the creams. What I should get was raw lanoline. It would be a bit tough, he said, to work into the skin, but it would not only prevent wrinkles, it would erase those already there. Not that I had any, he added.

I later got the raw lanoline, which proved to need a hydraulic drill to get into.

On his next visit, we talked about books and poetry. But still the stuff he had got from France before the fall hadn't done its job. I was feeling so ill now that I couldn't get up. On his fourth visit, he seemed a little concerned. 'This amazes me,' he said. 'It's always done the trick before. I would double the dose.'

I did, and the fall of France was repeated over again. It seemed at one point that if I didn't stand on my head, my intestines would drop out. Tom had to call the doctor in hurriedly.

He examined me again. 'My dear,' he said solemnly. 'You are pregnant.'

There were ships being sunk every day, their captains going down with them, yet there he was standing in that room. There was no justice.

I carried my baby for six months. I was nine days in labour. I should have gone to hospital, but they were bombing London – which was pretty near, and if anything was to happen I wanted to be with Tom – so I stuck it out in that little bedroom above the dispatch riders' office. When Tom helped deliver his son on Saturday, 7 December 1940, I was ready to die. And I could have because things went wrong inside.

There the ex-naval doctor was again, accompanied by another doctor. 'Just breathe in deeply, my dear,' he said.

When I woke up from the chloroform some time later, they told me I was swearing like any trooper. It was a pattern I was to repeat on waking from the many operations that were to follow. I, who would never use a swear word, not even a damn, bloodied and buggered all doctors and nurses ever after.

My mother's comment on my loss in her letter was merely to say, of Tom: 'Well he's proved himself.'

◆　◆　◆

I must recall a strange happening before I get on to the next doctor. It was when I was recovering from the loss of the baby, and also an electric

shock from picking up a wire-handled electric fire with a soapy hand –
the result of which was that I screamed in my head for days. So it was
almost three months later, in the spring of 1941, that Tom and I went
out for an evening walk.

The Latin master at the school knew a great deal about birds, and
it was this Mr Wright who aroused Tom's interest in bird life and told
him about a walk outside St Albans where he would see a number of
different species. This was why Tom proposed a gentle walk for me.

After being in bed for so long, my legs were rather wobbly and
as we entered a village, I recall saying, 'We'd better have a bus back.'
There was a country inn to the left, and behind it a deep drop as if into
a valley. We passed it and came to a sort of crossroads. There weren't
many people to be seen, but we stopped someone – I don't remember
if it was a man or a woman – and asked where we could get a bus back
to St Albans. There was a shaking of the head, but no response was
forthcoming, only a queer look.

Further on, we stopped a man and he said there was no bus that
went through their village, but if we took that path – he pointed – and
went past two farms, it would lead us to a main road. He too gave us a
queer look – as if we might be German spies, I thought.

I could hardly walk when we came to the first farm, but as we saw
no one about, we went on. The second farm was more like a manor
house. We knocked on the door and whoever answered said there was
no way to the main road except across the fields, and they were private,
but we could take that way if we were careful. They too looked at us as
if we were German spies.

By this time, Tom was practically carrying me and I was crying
from fatigue.

It was around half past six in the evening when we had set out,
and it was becoming dark, but there before us was the main road. Tom
got me over a fence and I collapsed into a ditch. A bus did come along
the road – it was empty and on its way to St Albans. The driver kindly

helped Tom to get me into it. Tom asked him the name of the village that we had come through: he couldn't tell us; that way wasn't his route. But he did say it couldn't have been such and such a village because that was about eight miles away.

I spent three days in bed, and for some part of each day I upbraided Tom for getting us lost.

When Tom enquired of Mr Wright about the village, he didn't seem to recall a place like that in walking distance from the town. Other enquiries brought similar remarks. About a month later, we took a bus to the outskirts of the town and walked along this road, noting how far we were going so we could return the same way. But, having walked twice the distance we did on that other night, there was no sign of the village and no one we spoke to could give us any information concerning it. A village was named with a pub in it, but when we saw it, it wasn't anything like the one we had passed through.

Why? If this thing had happened to me alone, I would have said it was a figment of my vivid imagination. But from when we first married I had recognised that Tom was the original doubting Thomas and sceptical about most things he couldn't prove through reason.

We still talk about it.

4

Tom was called up in 1941, and the chasm opened up in me again. I'd known loneliness before, but this feeling was devastating, overwhelming – and I was pregnant again. There was no need to question it this time.

As I said, there was a doctor right across the road from the flat, and I went to him. He was such a nice man: sympathetic and kindly. He warned me to take things easy and to be very careful, having lost my first baby.

When I heard on my return to St Albans some time later that he had committed suicide, I felt so sad. I'd only met him the once, but his kindness had left an impression on me. Why do these things happen so often? It's stupid to imagine that doctors shouldn't be ill, either mentally or physically, yet people do. They consider that, being medical men, they have the know-all to cure themselves.

After weeks of separation, Tom came home. It was such a wonderful reunion. I wrote pages about it; I still have them, but on reading they sound so sentimental – no one would believe the words came from me. My thoughts and feelings during those few days are very telling and give a much clearer picture of the two of us during that time. I hesitated at first about inserting the following because it is very personal and sentimental, yet what is life without sentiment?

It was written in pencil in an exercise book and went as follows:

First day, 15 February 1942

I'm pregnant again and I'm going to call him Valentine. Why Valentine?
I just don't know. The name suddenly came to me. Last night when I
was waiting for Tom to come, I knelt by my bed and said a decade of
the Rosary – the first decade, The Annunciation – and my mind kept
straying off the beads thinking, 'If I am to have a child, dear Lord, grant
that he will be healthy and good. Grant that there will never be any wars
for him to fight in. Give him his father's brains and his kind and sweet
disposition. Give him a strong sense of justice and tolerance. And, dear
Lord,' I said, apologetically with a smile, 'give him my sense of humour.'

At nine o'clock he came in, so tired, so dirty and so hungry. While
he held me tight and long in his arms I could only think, 'My dear,
my dear.' He would hold me at arm's length then pull me close to him
until I protested.

What a supper I had for him: rump steak (my whole week's ration),
bacon and sausages, fried bread, then a trifle. But he didn't eat as much
as I wanted him to. I think he was so excited at seeing me – yet it isn't
three weeks since he went away but it has seemed such a long time. An
eternity to us both.

After supper, we sat by the fire in that little kitchen and talked of
many things. Why he didn't take his commission in armaments. Was
he sure of being made an instructor in wireless? The awful dumps they
were billeted in and, of course, the war. When would it end? I didn't
say to him what I was thinking – what I had thought so often – that
it didn't matter to me for I always had this weird feeling that I would
never see the end of the war. No matter how I reasoned with myself, I
still imagined I would never see the end of it. This wasn't brought on by
the feeling of depression I had had since Tom had joined up in August.
I had had it since the very beginning of the war. And in a strange way,
I didn't see the end of it – at least I wasn't aware of it. But, of course,
I didn't say anything; I just let him talk about The Hurst and what we

would do when we went back. He became quite serious about having the lawn made into flower beds and I, quite as seriously, decided against his suggestion. 'For where,' I asked him, 'would we get the time to look after eighty feet of flowers?' We couldn't keep the grounds tidy as it was. And all the time thinking, 'What did it matter?'

And then we went to bed. The pleasure I got from seeing him stretching his five foot five and a half inches and exclaim, 'Oh, darling, sheets.' He lay in my arms quietly like a child making little grunting noises, which he always does when he's happy. He talked at intervals saying silly things such as, I was the most beautiful woman in the world. That out of all of God's creatures, there wasn't one to compare with me, and never in his wildest dreams had he thought to get anyone like me for a wife. A dream come to life. He said it hesitantly for words don't come to him easily. Of course, it wasn't true, but I was touched and pleased. Then I made him happy and I lay in his arms and he stroked my hair to send me off to sleep as he always does, and I forgot everything but the warmth of his body. Then it was morning.

I was awake first. I did not move but lay as if still asleep, thinking, 'Had my baby begun? Really begun?' Then for a moment I was terrified at the thought that it just might have begun, but only for a moment. What was there to be afraid of? Nothing would happen to me this time – it mustn't. He would miss me so and nothing must happen to make him as desolate as he would be without me. He needed me; I was the strength behind all he did. I was his urge to do. I was the cloak that covered his shyness and timidity. I was the stimulus to that fine brain. I was his life. Without me he would just sink back into the nice, quiet little fellow: lonely and lost. No, nothing must happen to me. Yet what about the gnawing thought that I wouldn't live to see the end of the war?

He stirred and said, 'Awake, dearest?' He gathered me into his arms and I snuggled close to him and there we lay, talking at intervals for another hour. At nine o'clock, he got up and lit the fire and brought me a cup of tea. It was so like old times. Then I got up and made breakfast and asked him if he would like to go to Mass with me. He said yes, but I felt he didn't want to move from the fire so I said, 'It's too late now for eleven o'clock, anyway, as I have to get the dinner on and get ready.' It wasn't, and I felt it was wrong of me to miss Mass – it seemed very thankless after my prayers had been answered and him right here beside me. But he had been so tired and so cold in the past three weeks and he looked so comfortable that I would have done anything rather than disturb him. So I cooked the dinner and tidied up and he pottered about. It was as if we had never heard of war; we were back in the past that might have been but that we had never known together – a time of ordinary married life. How suburban but how wonderful. And as dinner time approached, it was hard to believe that in a few hours he would be gone.

When he pulled down all his books that he had stacked so carefully away in the clothes cupboard and strew them all over the passage in search of a maths book, I pretended to go for him. 'All right, darling. All right, darling. I'm going to put them all back in a jiffy.' There they lay for two hours while he looked at this book and that. 'He will never grow up,' I thought. 'There's so much of the boy in him. The boy who must go on learning in order that he can pass his knowledge, especially of mathematics, onto others.'

The train was to leave at four fifty and we left the flat at four thirty. When we ran into the Warship Week procession we thought we had plenty of time and stood and watched a while. 'The RAF is the smartest lot,' he said. 'Of course, naturally,' I replied. But it was true, they were. And then we nearly missed the train. We just jumped in as it was going and I hadn't a ticket. We laughed as if we had done something clever. Tom had to stand; he needn't have, but the girl with the skin coat who sat in the corner had placed herself very comfortably sideways and not one of my light hints caused her to flicker an eyelid, much less move her legs.

We had two hours to wait at King's Cross. The train left at seven fifteen, and as there was one leaving St Pancras at the same time that would get me into St Albans shortly after eight, he wouldn't let me stay to see him off. I felt in the depths of misery when I left him. He stood outside the side entrance to King's Cross and I kept turning round and waving but I couldn't really see him for the dusk and my tears.

I sat in the corner of the compartment and cried, and a woman opposite me looked at me through her heavy lids – such an animal stare; not even curiosity. Then, without warning, my nose started to bleed. I felt that hot wave of fear that bleeding always brings and the thick smell of blood, but it wasn't much and for that I was sincerely thankful, for one of those awful bleedings in my present state would have been the last straw. During it all, the lady continued to stare at me without speaking.

When I got out of the train, I was cold and miserable. I felt so down. I decided to call in at Mrs Fowler's next door for I couldn't face that lonely flat tonight by myself. Mrs Fowler put the news on and Churchill spoke.

I had thought it was impossible for me to feel more depressed. But as, in his grand way, Churchill told us of the fall of Singapore, I sank into the depths of my being. I thought of the wives and the mothers who would be heartsick at this moment – their men out there, their men who they might never see again. And again, there went up a silent prayer in thanks that my husband was just at Cranwell. Yet, my reason asked, why should God favour one in preference to another? In times of trouble I fight my faith with reason but my faith often wins.

So the first day of Valentine's being came to an end. But why am I so sure his being began?

Second day, 16 February 1942

This morning I lay in bed thinking of yesterday and talking to Valentine. It was silly of me, but so what if it was? Who was there to know or criticise? I don't think I'm particularly fond of the name Valentine. I would rather have David, but then David died. He didn't get the chance of a life. I wonder if God looks after babies of six months? I absolutely refuse to believe that they go to limbo. It's just about a year ago that Tom took me to see his grave. I remember how sick I felt when the man told me he was in a general grave together with three men and an old woman whom I gathered had come from the Union. He wasn't allowed a grave because he wasn't baptised. I felt so indignant for he had looked so sweet the first and only time I saw him. Then I thought the old woman would look after him and she'll be so pleased to find a baby with her . . . Fanciful, but it helped to ease the hurt, which in itself was exaggerated owing to my weak state at the time.

And how wonderful Tom was to me during all those awful weeks of illness. How he worked before he went to school, and then again when he returned with never a cross word or murmur. But that is Tom.

There will be no letter from him today but he is to phone tonight. I hope he gets through early for I don't like to intrude myself on the Fowlers. How worried I get if I don't get a letter every day. I imagine the wildest things: he's dead, he's been run over, he's been accidentally shot, the policeman is knocking at the door to bring me the news. I am stunned, the world is empty, I can't go on. To think that I will never see him again . . . It's all very real until that sensible side of me says in a cold voice with a big hint of derision, 'Come on, Katie, snap out of it.'

The news has been on; they think there are nearly 60,000 men left in Singapore. Dear God! How terrible. Sixty thousand women crying this night all over the world with agony in their hearts not knowing if their men are dead or alive. That is the worst – the gnawing anxiety of uncertainty. God help and comfort them at this hour.

Third day, 17 February 1942

I've had a dreadful night. Tom didn't phone last night. I waited until nine thirty. In fact long after I had outstayed my welcome – at least so I felt, but I'm hypersensitive about intruding.

When at last I came upstairs, I was sick with a dread feeling I usually get when anything goes wrong concerning Tom. If I had known he had arrived safely I would not have minded so much. So all night I tossed and turned and dreamed dreadful dreams.

His promised letter came this morning and as it was written yesterday morning he didn't give the reason for not phoning, but it was so sweet. Just a hurried note written before he had to fly to breakfast and after he had cleaned the wash houses out . . . Tom cleaning wash houses . . . He doesn't mind, he says. They've all got to do it. But it makes me wild: he with his fine mathematical brain being used to clean wash houses and latrines. But there are many such cases. Will we win the war with square pegs in round holes? Many doubt it. They spoke of it on the broadcast to schools this morning, which was strange.

In his letter he said, 'What a grand weekend I've had, dearest one. Really, darling, it was just too wonderful for words to see that look in your eyes when I opened the door. It was like an invitation to paradise. And so it was. All the unhappiness that had been growing in me fell away completely and I was again in my beloved's arms; I was again kissing her beautiful face and her voice was playing the most wonderful music in my ears. Dearest, if I could only write down words sufficient to tell you just a little of how much I love you then I should be satisfied – I try but can find nothing with which to compare it. I have a little body but my heart seems to swell right out of it when I'm with you.'

On and on he writes, so beautifully, yet he hates writing letters. He says he has no imagination; he really thinks so, and he really thinks that I am beautiful. Perhaps my body, yes, but my face is much too stiff and my look is often unfortunately haughty, and my glasses and green eyes don't help much, but when I smile it covers a lot of defects. But one can't be always smiling. Still, if he retains enough imagination to always think I am beautiful then I ask no more.

Fourth day, 18 February 1942

He did not phone last night. Oh, how I prayed that there was nothing wrong with him, and then this morning his letter came; a most beautiful letter, telling me that it was impossible for him to phone on Monday night as he had to line up for two hours for a new jacket, and when at last he got to the phone box he was informed that it would be eleven o'clock before he could get through and lights were out at ten thirty. He was so worried for he knew how worried I would be. He said a lot of things about the RAF's organisation. He went on to say, 'Not until I entered these gates last night did the old dreadful feeling of having my hands tied behind my back and a gag thrust into my mouth come over me again. All the while previously, coming back from London, I was living the weekend over again in my head, but then these gates just seemed to spell hell once more.'

He goes on to tell me that he thinks about me once again. I become embarrassed at times that anyone should think of me in this light. Then he says, 'The wonderful weekend you have given me has furthered more than ever my belief in a God . . . It seems funny, doesn't it, but just think that I admit it and you'll realise what a change I have undergone. I really wanted to go to Mass yesterday morning for I have prayed so hard lately and I think I have prayed fervently. I'll go on praying for you, my darling. Praying that neither physical nor mental harm should come to you; praying that you might always be happy, that you'll get all you deserve. I always tell Our Lady that you are so good and that you deserve so much. I should not use the word deserve for She knows best how She intercedes for you. She knows what I mean. To a certain extent it makes me feel easier in my mind to think that I can talk to Her and through Her to you. You know that I would never have said I felt like this unless I really did. Perhaps it seems a big transformation to you, but certain things can happen in a flash. Actually, in my case, it has been a comparatively gradual transition and it has all been through you.

It did seem funny to me to think how much prayer meant to you, but now I know, sweetheart, and I have to thank you for showing me. As I might have said one time, I haven't gone soft. I'm still the same person, but there's just something different behind it all. It was born with the realisation of how you loved me. That I should be given the great love for you and to know that it was reciprocated just had to have something behind it. Oh, my sweetheart, you are divine, as divine as you'll ever be even after death. I just think of you as being as big in heart and mind, as big in giving, as big in everything that matters in life for me. Some people are born great, some achieve greatness and some have greatness thrust upon them. I was neither born the first nor achieved the second, but I know it has come my way to be taken into the arms of a great love. There may I die.'

So, Valentine, that's your father, but the picture he draws isn't your mother, just as he imagines her to be. Is love blind or has it a thousand eyes? I don't know, but this I do know: no one could ever be as good or as beautiful as he imagines me to be, and I also know that there is no one as good as he. There was one time he did not believe in God, or even in the possibility of there being a God, and I never thought that I should alter him. I did not want to then – that was when we first met in 1937. For the previous seven years, I had given no thought to God myself or the Catholic religion I had come to criticise openly. God forgive me, and for the thoughts that I still harbour – namely that there are a lot of flaws in religion, but still that isn't God's fault, it's man's. And are they flaws or is it that I don't want to accept a rigid standard of living? Perhaps it is so, but one thing I do hate, Valentine, is the business of paid pews. In Leicester, at that beautiful Church of the Holy Cross – beautiful in a non-Catholic way for I have never seen a Catholic church like it, nor heard such a flow of fine modulated language from the pulpit: a cross between a Bernard Shaw and H.G. Wells – there you cannot see the Mass except out of one eye and this you do at the risk of a crick in your neck because all the seats facing the altar are paid seats with private cassocks. Very fine those cassocks: nice and thick so the knees of the great won't crack. How I wanted to crack their necks for them many a Sunday morning during my four-month stay in Leicester. How enraged I used to get at the smugness of those strange people for the most part with cars waiting outside and petrol that perhaps cost the lives of a hundred sailors. One Sunday morning, I imagined those sailors standing round those cars waiting for their owners. Oh, if only it could have been possible. But as beautiful as the church was, it left me without that warm feeling – the feeling that I get in this gaudy little church here. But I think this is mainly due to the priest who can talk like H.G. Wells, but in his coarse, Irish, booming voice gives you his heart, tells you the goodness of people not the badness, doesn't frighten you with hell, but talks of God's mercy, and even talks of the good non-Catholics – how the Leicester priests would argue with him on that point. By the way, he isn't the first priest I came across in St Albans, the one who said Mass when Tom first accompanied me there. This one spoke of hellfire and brimstone and said it was no symbol but reality and that everyone who went to hell was made to sit on burning gridirons. I don't know how I looked at Tom or explained that priest's views; all I know is he almost threw me back into my seven-year isolation.

Fifth day, 19 February 1942

Tom phoned last night; how far away and lost he sounded. He didn't seem well, but it was wonderful to hear him. He said quite a lot that I couldn't catch. What I did hear was, 'Do you love me?'

Do I love him? Do I miss him? Oh, this lonely life; so aimless without him.

I feel more certain you are coming, Valentine, and with you life will not be so lonely, but in a fortnight's time I will have to register. I feel I should do something, but then if you are here you will, I know, floor me for a time. But you have a lot in your favour for I am much stronger than I was when David was coming.

That first year of the war with ten blind evacuees and mental patients in the house was too much on top of the hard work and nerve strain of the previous years – ten of them spent with mental defectives. Not that I disliked them – very much to the contrary, that's why I found them so easy to handle – but the nerve strain left its mark nevertheless.

Do you know, Valentine, in June it will be two years since Tom and I were married, yet it seems a happy lifetime ago. I can't look back to a time when we weren't together, so completely has he wiped out all the past from my mind. I loved him when I married him, but compared to the feelings I have for him now, that was but a blade of grass compared to a great plain. His goodness, his kindness, his humility, his very need of me, have all piled themselves on top of one another and become the great, amazing, consuming feeling that is within me.

Sixth day, 20 February 1942

He isn't well. His letter this morning says he has a terrific cold and that he coughed for hours last night. I thought he wasn't well. If only I could be near him to doctor him and make a fuss of him . . . Oh, this war. And now the Japs are swarming like ants over Burma, only 1000 miles from Australia. The battle in Libya is like a see-saw: first we take a place then we lose it, then we take it again. Backward and forward over burning sands, hundreds of miles of it. How the men must long for the end of it all. But it must seem easier to count the grains of sand than see the end. Only Russia seems to be moving in the right direction. Grant that they may never stop.

It is six thirty and I'm sitting by the fire; everything looks bright and clean, the furniture is shining, the brasses are gleaming, it is so comfortable, yet he is not here to enjoy it. He is in a cold, wooden hut and he is not well.

We don't ask much of life, only to be together, but isn't that what thousands of couples are saying at this moment? Anyway, I should thank God for him being in a wooden hut; many of those abroad would give anything to be in his place. But my heart is crying out against it all, for all he wants to do is to teach his boys and come home to me. And all I want is for him to come home to me. Such a little to ask of life. But we are at war . . . How he wanted to get into it, to feel he was doing something. He was torn between the fact of leaving me and doing his duty and now he is feeling he is doing absolutely nothing: simply the victim of red tape.

He longs to be back: once again taking the boys, once again going to the matches on a Saturday afternoon, once again experiencing the grumbles in the common room, once again doing monthly reports, once again games meetings where nobody agrees, once again the same monotonous round that would be so wonderful.

Seventh day, 21 February 1942

Today I feel very dull, Valentine. I suppose it's because a week ago today I was so excited at him coming home. I had to do my shopping just the same but without the same urge. And let it be noted, last week I fell down in the street and ripped a pair of perfectly good silk stockings. It didn't matter about cutting my knee or shaking myself up but to tear beyond repairing a pair of whole silk stockings was a tragedy. But today nothing like that happened. I walked very sedately; I didn't want to pat children's heads, or smile at bus conductors – female or otherwise. And now I don't want to tap dance to the wireless or talk ridiculous nonsense to Tom as he sits framed in the picture above my head. There he is in the second row of a football team, his Oxford scarf making him look like a tough guy. I'm firmly convinced that one day he'll burst out laughing at the silly things I say, but I have seen him look sad when I cried in front of that picture when I haven't had a letter.

I went to the pictures this afternoon and I did laugh. I do like to laugh, Valentine, right out, heartily, uproariously. In the pictures, I sometimes go on laughing after everyone else has stopped. Now, your father laughs silently, or nearly so – he shakes and gets a pain. But we both laugh and enjoy the same things, which is a very great thing, for imagine telling your husband something you think is really funny and him meeting it with a deadpan face. I, for my part, would never attempt it again. That would mean keeping all the fun in life to oneself. I should imagine it would go sour on you.

Eighth day, 22 February 1942

What makes a Sunday so different? Even if you don't go to church it's different. Is it because you lie in bed longer? But then I can lie in bed any morning I like. But the bedroom looks different on a Sunday. I look out of the window at the policeman on guard outside the police station opposite: he looks Sunday morningish. He doesn't look so smart; he looks more at ease than he did yesterday. He claps his hands together to keep them warm – not a thing he would do on a Wednesday or a Saturday, I'm sure. A seagull perches on the air raid siren right above his head. That seagull is a long way from its wet pastures, but as it wobbles backward and forward it seems to say, 'Who cares? It's Sunday.'

I went to Communion at nine o'clock, but on the way I couldn't get my mind into the right groove. Other people were on their way to different churches all in their Sunday best and it set me thinking. I never keep Sunday best. I like to be smart every day and something inside me – I suppose it's my very contrary side that always wants to appear different – kicks against the stuffy idea of Sunday best. Why not wear the best you have on a Tuesday afternoon or a Friday morning? Think of the pleasure you get out of your clothes and their effect on your mind – for undoubtedly it is a tonic of no small value to feel well dressed.

In this state of mind, I went to church. Once there, I had so many things to ask my friend that I soon forgot about the dress, and after taking Communion, I told Him that dress would be of no value whatsoever if I could have kept Him with me all the time as I felt Him at that moment.

But there – God's a very busy person.

Later, I went to tea at the Fowlers'. Tom did not phone. I was so disappointed.

Ninth day, 23 February 1942

Monday. Tom's letter this morning was merely a hurried note – he had been put on cooking duties and hadn't a minute to himself – but it was a sweet note.

I worked as usual all morning. How does a flat get so dusty when there's only me in it? Still, I liked cleaning it. This afternoon I went to see Elsie and Doris Waters in a picture, the name of which I have forgotten. I didn't really enjoy it because of the man with the fishy smell. He sat next to me just as this picture started and the first waft of him turned my stomach. It was terrible. He had to make matters worse because he was wearing scent and the combination nearly made me sick. If there had been another seat I would have taken it, even at the risk of hurting his feelings. That's a thing I don't like to do – move away from a stranger, especially on a bus. Unless, of course, he or she is really objectionable. I always feel slighted when anyone on a bus moves away from me to another seat and I hate to see it done to anyone else. I always feel like going up to the one who's left and patting them and saying, 'It's all right. They only wanted to look out of the window. That was the reason they left you.' And I can always see them smiling, assured in themselves once more, saying, 'Oh, thank you.'

Tenth day, 24 February 1942

He's coming home again on Saturday, Valentine. He did some slight service for his flight sergeant and another pass was his reward. I would love to kiss that sergeant. It seems too good to be true. What will I give him to eat? I'll get a tin of peas with my points and some lamb chops and they may have some dates in. He loves dates. Will I have enough points? Oh, I feel so excited again.

Eleventh day, 25 February 1942

Today I washed all the chair covers and clothes. Mrs Fowler let me wash them in her machine. It was a big help but very tiring, and when I came upstairs again my fire was out and I had to hurry and get my dinner and write to Tom and get ready for two forty-five for Mrs Fowler was calling for me. We were going to a ladies' afternoon in the Methodist church round the corner.

Now, I don't like women's afternoons or ladies' afternoons or any place where a crowd of women gather together for a talk. I've heard it all before and suffered from it. But Mrs Fowler has been so nice to me and she has been to one of these meetings and enjoyed it so I thought it would seem rather discourteous to refuse, and again she might think it was because I was a Catholic. So I went, and there in a tiny room were about fifty women – quite nice women. They all looked at me when I went in, but they were kind looks, and when the meeting was over their leader – an insignificant little woman to look at – came over and spoke to me. I told her right away that I was a Catholic. She replied, 'Aren't we all?' And here's a funny thing, although I admired the way she spoke, I didn't like her. There was something about her. She was a little busy bee no doubt, but a determined one. I'm going to the top of the hive little busy bee.

Perhaps I don't like bees.

Thinking of bees, Mrs Bean, our old landlady, was there. She was surprised to see me. She's a very good-living woman – I liked her.

Twelfth day, 26 February 1942

Darling, I feel so upset. No Valentine. Not yet, anyway. Oh, I'm disappointed. So very, very disappointed. But there'll be another time; there must, there must.

◆ ◆ ◆

When Tom told me he was being sent to Cranwell [an RAF station in Lincolnshire] for officer training, I was determined to follow him. I let the flat with the proviso that I could, at times, use the sitting room when passing through. The tenants were a young couple, so sanctimonious they had their apartments already booked upstairs. Why was I worrying? she said. If anything happened to my husband, he would go straight to heaven if he had been a good man. No, she said, she would never worry about her husband being killed.

She was about twenty-five years old. I've met a number like her since. One, a lady doctor, said to her patient who had lost her baby, 'You mustn't cry, woman – your child's in heaven with the angels.' She also said a similar thing to a man who had just lost his wife. The wife happened to be a friend of mine.

By the way, I was pregnant again.

I booked in at a small hotel in Sleaford, then set about trying to find rooms. An old lady who had let her big house off in apartments to servicemen's wives took pity on me. Although she couldn't find me a spot in her own house, she knew of a woman who had a room to let. I was prepared to be grateful for anything, but when I saw that room my gratitude failed me, for it beat even my experience of the landladies' orange box apartments in Hastings. It had a big iron bed with a mattress shaped like the Alps; as for the bedding, I wouldn't have put it under my dogs. Tom was a bit shattered by the sight of the room too, but it didn't matter: we were together and we could laugh about it.

To get to the little kitchen, I had to pass through the living room. My landlady had trouble with her bladder, and every morning she informed me of this. 'How are you feeling this morning?' I would ask. 'Oh, me dear, it's the neck of me bladder again,' she would reply without variation.

I was feeling ill, so once again I sought out a doctor and again I was lucky, for he was a very nice and thoughtful man. I had to go very careful, he said, and rest as much as possible.

One night, Tom came home to tell me that he was being given a week's leave – that was the usual transition from being a corporal to an officer. I can see myself now, begging him to refuse the commission. Something told me that he must refuse that commission, while at the same time I knew he would be the only one of the masters who had been called up to be in the ranks. But if I wanted him to live, he must refuse that commission. He had been training in wireless, so I said, 'Tell them you want to stay on the educational side.'

It must have taken a great deal for him to do as I asked, but he did it, and uncomplainingly. The result in the following years was that, when twice he was put forward for a commission, it was refused him. And that's how I wanted it. I think I had become slightly psychic where Tom was concerned – perhaps it was through my passionate love for him.

I first experienced this when he joined up while he was in Yarmouth doing his square-bashing. It was the night before I was travelling to Leicester to meet up with him that I woke up in fear and trembling. I had seen the bombs dropping along a seafront and the corpses being wheeled away. It was around three in the morning, and I sat up for the rest of the night. He was waiting for me at the station in Leicester, and within a short time of our meeting he confirmed my dream. There had been a raid, and they had dropped incendiary bombs all along the front and machine-gunned it. He had been on duty with two other men, one of whom had not been so lucky . . .

But to return to Sleaford. Two days before Tom was to be posted to Hereford, the doctor was called in.

'My dear,' he said. 'I'm afraid you're going to lose your baby. In fact, you're losing it.'

Tom had to leave on Friday morning. My landlady, her husband and son were going off on holiday on the Sunday – funny this: they could run a car, yet the underclothes she put on the line had to be seen to be believed, for they represented the clearest poverty; the frugality of their living, too, had to be witnessed. But they had their holiday booked. So I had to get out of that bed and be on my way before they left on the Sunday morning.

On Saturday, I couldn't get out of that bed; I was in a fever. The doctor came again. I hadn't lost my baby, but I would have to go into hospital in Grantham.

There I was at seven o'clock in the evening heading in an ambulance for Grantham, where I was put to bed and a young nurse was told to get me ready for the theatre.

This was in March 1942 and there were a lot of volunteers drafted in to do all kinds of work. It was one such who was detailed to deal with me, for I'm sure she had never shaved anyone in her life before. I was used to rough treatment and tried not to call out – I just cringed and squirmed. But when the sister saw her charge's handiwork, it was she who almost screamed. 'Why didn't you go ahead and perform an operation?' she cried. 'And look, you've made her nose bleed an' all – you've seen to back, top and bottom, I'll say you have.'

That poor nurse. In her defence, I told the sister that my nose bled frequently; in fact, it bled somewhat every day. She didn't believe me.

It was about nine o'clock at night when I was put on a trolley and pushed towards the theatre, only to be stopped halfway. They were bringing in the victims of an accident just outside the hospital.

I lay on that trolley in a side corridor until almost twelve o'clock, when at last I was wheeled into the theatre. The sight of the blood-bespattered doctors and the smell almost finished me, but a smiling face bent over me and drew his fingers across the ruching of my nightie, saying, 'By, that's a nice nightie you've got on.' As I was supposed to be an emergency, that poor nurse hadn't taken my nightie off, just covered it with a white smock.

◆ ◆ ◆

Even though she does not mention it specifically, it seems likely that Catherine lost another baby that evening in March.

◆ ◆ ◆

The next day, the face appeared above me again, saying, 'Now you must rest for a few days, a week at least, and it would be advisable not to attempt any more children. In fact, you mustn't have any more. You understand?'

I didn't at that time. But what I did understand was I wasn't staying there a week. Tom was in Hereford; he had got rooms for us, and that was where I was going. Three days later, I had to sign a paper saying I was leaving of my own free will.

I have omitted to mention when I first followed the air force and landed in Leicester at the house of a Mrs Grant. I think the time we spent with her was the happiest of our wartime experiences of land-ladies. Tom was allowed to sleep out, but not with his wife – it was immoral – so he was billeted in the next street, having to share a bed with another man, which nearly drove him up the pole. There was a baby in the house, and to watch the child being treated in such a way, it's a wonder it survived – if ever it did. Tom loves children, and this young baby was wrapped up to the eyes and changed about once a day.

Every night, there was a card-and-beer session, when the family would sit round the table and one or other would run with the cans for beer. He always escaped to Mrs Grant's, and it became the expected thing that he slept there.

It was during this period that I felt I must do something towards the war effort, so offered to help with the parcels to prisoners. That effort lasted four days.

Why, I kept asking myself, did I always feel so ill? Perhaps it was the worry over Tom. This was the main thing, but there were others too. I was beginning to worry about my birth too – the words illegitimate and bastard could disturb me, I found – and I was searching for the answer as to why I'd been such a fool to put up with Nan Smith all those years. And then there was our Kate, my mother. My feelings for her ranged from tenderness to hatred. And threaded through everything was this thing called reason, which had been attacking the Catholic faith for years and which now seemed to get stronger each day.

When I left Grantham Hospital, I knew I wasn't fit enough to make the journey to Hereford, and so I got in touch with Mrs Grant and asked her if I could stay overnight.

Of course, someone else was in our room (I thought of it as our room). She kept that house so clean, so spotless, yet the floor of one of the bedrooms upstairs was almost dropping through, and there was one lavatory outside so that we had to wait our turn. Her Bill was in South Africa and her little boy was born when we were there. She was kind to me: she gave me her bed, and I've never forgotten that. I tried to get in touch with her after the war – I wrote, but she didn't reply.

The next day, I went on to Hereford.

There was no one at the station to meet me. I took a taxi to Ryelands Street, a highly respectable quarter. I was shown our sitting room and bedroom, which were very nice indeed. As I'd had nothing to eat all day, I asked if I could make a drink. I put a pan of milk on the stove in the spotless kitchen and let it boil over. I had straightaway blotted my copy book.

5

The three years I spent in Hereford were the unhappiest of my life. It was as if my life up to that point had been a sore boil and in that town, it burst. Even now, the thought of the place chills me. I could never visit there, ever. Yet it was in that town that two of my talents ripened. I had started to draw in St Albans. In Hereford, it went apace. I found I could do faces as well as cathedrals. My landlady's father was a retired railwayman; he was a very nice old man, so quiet. I made him laugh – strange, I always wanted to make people laugh, while inside I was fighting my miseries. I used to rant about causes, and this used to amuse him. As he had said to Tom, he had never met anyone like me.

I remember my excessive indignation over a separate bus being provided for the ladies of the officers when invited to a dance at Madley [a nearby village], and another put on for the wives of lesser mortals, including sergeants and corporals – who were considered less than dustmen. I raged about this class differentiation. Hadn't I lived in a gentlemen's residence, which I owned through a building society? Hadn't I been one of the highest-paid workers in Hastings Workhouse for ten years? But apart from all that, wasn't I the wife of a grammar schoolmaster? How dare they differentiate.

I can recall the tears running down the old man's cheeks. Of course, when I knew I was giving amusement I always let it rip – that was the clown in me.

Day after day, when on my own, I drew or wrote. My sitting-room window faced the street, and opposite I would see a very large woman doing her steps daily. I imagined she was in her fifties. At this time, I was getting good likenesses with my two pencils, academy chalk and carbon crayon. I asked her to sit for me. She was delighted . . . until she saw the result, which was the dead spit of her. We didn't even exchange greetings after that. Anyway, my landlady and the fat lady's family weren't on speaking terms. The camaraderie of the war hadn't reached Ryelands Street.

My landlady was a school teacher and had a seven-year-old son. John was very fond of Tom, and whenever possible would come into our room. I wrote stories for him, and when he was put to bed I would often slip into his room to try to stop him rocking himself, which he did incessantly until he fell asleep. John grew to be a fine boy and a well-liked scout, but he died when he was fourteen of leukaemia.

My landlady's husband was in the air force like Tom, but was stationed some distance away. Yet he risked being nabbed almost every weekend in order to return home for a few hours. He was a very good-looking man and deeply in love with his wife.

Tom had to travel seven miles every morning to Madley and seven miles back at night. If he was five minutes late, I would get onto my knees and pray. Looking back on my emotional state, it's a wonder the boil didn't burst sooner.

Never a day passed that I didn't feel ill, but my conscience was pricking me: everybody was doing their bit except me. I was exempt because of ill health, but I felt sure that there were other people worse than me at work. So I went into the munitions factory on the outskirts of the town and sat at the table with a number of women in a shed and rammed cordite into cases. All the time observing the waste of labour owing to the set-up of the building and the timidity of the overseer. I, who had been getting work out of reluctant staff and inmates for fifteen years, became quietly enraged at the dodging and the slow output in my shed.

Of course, I let off steam in the evenings about this and again amused my landlady's father, Mr Smith. I became so indignant about the waste of manpower – or womanpower in this case – that I took advantage of the notice pinned on the office board on improving output.

I wrote out a schedule that would increase the work by one third. I did a diagram of the rearrangement of the shed on the principle that when women are stuck together at one table, they chatter. I suggested a competitive basis. I finished up by asking that if this method should be adopted, my name should be withheld – I didn't want to be lynched.

I was only on half-time and finished at one o'clock. One day, as I made my way back to our lodgings, I collapsed in the street and woke up in a strange house. It was the first time I had actually passed out. I remember coming up through layers of blackness, which recalled the nightmare dream I used to have as a child about going down into hell. An ambulance took me back to my digs, to the surprise of my landlady. I'm sure in those days I was a kind of weird oddity to her. Some people cannot stand illness – they're afraid of it, and very often it is people who have never really been ill who shy from it in others. I did not find her of a very sympathetic nature, to say the least.

The following morning, I got an official letter from the War Office offering me a managerial job in an ammunition works in the Midlands. I had let myself in for something, hadn't I: following Tom all around the country only to be sent to the Midlands. But fortune was on my side, as I had contracted cordite poisoning, to add to the lead poisoning.

◆　◆　◆

When did I become pregnant again? I've lost touch of the dates. Tom was in a state as I'd been warned not to let it happen. I was constantly bleeding from the nose and tongue – and then there was the cordite poisoning. But I was determined to have a baby. When I had the house to myself, I sang. Moreover, I was now a commercial artist and doing drawings for J. Arthur Dixon of the Shanklin Press, Isle of Wight. That came about by fluke, as I have explained elsewhere. All of the artists were at war and they were looking under the bottom of barrels – that's how I got my chance.

Now and again, we would entertain some of Tom's pals who were instructors alongside him in Madley – Joe Raine, Joe Golding and Reg Greatorex. I did sketches of them. It was one of the few pleasant times I experienced in that town.

Then one morning, I was on my knees doing the hearth when I felt a click in my side. I gasped, covered my face with my hands and rocked myself like a Muslim at prayer, crying inside, '*Oh, no, no. Please God, no.*' But yes, I was to lose the third.

In hospital, just before they took me down, I said to the sister, 'Sister, I . . . I have the habit of swearing when I come out of chloroform. Will you please put me where nobody can hear me?' I can see her throwing her head back and laughing as she said, 'No, I won't. We want some entertainment here, and we only get that kind from parsons or priests.'

Following the loss, I became very low in myself. I was always tired and had a constant feeling of illness on me. I was also becoming full of self-pity for this girl who hadn't a father. Nothing that had happened to me would have happened if only I'd had a father. I recall trying to laugh myself out of it and saying, 'Well, you must have had – you're no relation to the Holy Mother.'

There were one or two light moments I can recall about that time. One was when I met one of the women from the munitions factory. She had the loudest mouth and the slowest hands on her long table. 'Oh, Mrs Cookson,' she said. 'You wouldn't like it back there now. You wouldn't be able to stand it. Everything's changed.' Then she went on to describe the plan I'd sent in. I gurgled inside while sympathising with her . . .

Religion was rearing its superstitious head again too. Was I being made ill because I was questioning the Catholic faith?

I went to the surgery. The doctor who saw me was youngish. If I remember rightly, he wasn't English and was of an impatient nature. He had no time for women he termed neurotic and who cried in his surgery.

I will diverge here.

It was about this time that I had to go back to Hastings to see to The Hurst. In those days, once you left Hereford, travelling was dangerous, as London was a shambles and Hastings was getting it too. I had been home, as I still called The Hurst, on one previous occasion when we were in St Albans, after a neighbour who had been keeping an eye on the house said he would no longer be responsible for it because Mrs Smith was taking away stacks of linen and things on a barrow. At the time, and for practically all the war, Nan Smith was stationed near Elphinstone Mount, taking in boarders from the pay corps up the road. She wanted their money and, also, that was likely why she needed the linen from the house.

But on this occasion, I was forced to go back to Hastings to clear up the effects of a time bomb that had shattered the observatory. What a pity it hadn't blown the house to bits. It would have saved a lot of trouble . . . Yet I loved that house. Anyway, I went down to Nan's, where I was to stay the night – with dire consequences.

She had a cold and, being on leave, was in bed. I happened to go into the kitchen where my one-time cook, now supposedly the housekeeper, Mrs Webster, was reigning. She was deaf, and the most ineffectual person I ever came across. I had taken her from the workhouse because she begged me for work. It was either that or going back into the Salvation Army in London. I found, to my cost, she could even burn water, but she was an expert at making the most delicate sandwiches and finger-rolled brown bread. Where she had learned this, I don't know, for she seemed to have been in an institution all her life. Yet she had a vivid imagination and said she had been married and had children. She was about six foot one with a gaunt, horse-looking face and hair that stood up as if in continual fright – a weird-looking creature altogether. Looking back, I realise I brought a lot of trouble on myself through my compassion and pity – both of these qualities have caused havoc in my life.

Mrs Webster was smoking as usual, and the sink was full of dishes. There was a great hunk of cheese and butter on the table, and I spied part of a ham in the cupboard.

This was evidence that Nan was up to her old what's-yours-is-mine tricks again . . . and the army was fair bait for everybody. She was regimental quartermaster sergeant and, as always, had a lot of friends. Nan always picked the influential ones, though I didn't realise this for a long time. In the army they were officers, and in civilian life they had been doctors and solicitors. They all gathered around dear old Nan, because there was no denying she had charm, and she always held her hand out freely to give what she had taken from someone else with both hands. For the previous nine years, the person she had taken from had been me. But now it was the army.

I went upstairs and into Nan's bedroom, and said something to the effect that the kitchen looked like Paddy's market and Mrs Webster was sitting amid rations that would feed a company.

At this, the woman who had been a scrubber in Hastings Workhouse Hospital and who had applied for work in my laundry when the only vacancy was pushing trolleys of wet linen and shaking clothes out ready for the calender, went for me. And as she did so, I remembered my first impression of her.

I had taken a strong dislike to Nan at the beginning, for once my back was turned she could stop others working by telling them some tale to make them laugh. Then came the time when I was doing the assistant matron's work during the flu epidemic and, coming into my office, Nan said to me, 'I know you don't like me, Miss Mac, but none of your staff want to do the night work. If you'll give me the chance, I'll just show you what I'm made of.'

And she did. She worked like two people for weeks and her charm worked on me – for a time. But here she was at this moment sitting up and yelling at me, 'Don't you dare go down and give orders to *my cook*. This is *my house*' – it wasn't, it was mine – 'and you can get yourself out of it. Who do you think you are?'

I'd had years of worry, years of fear of what she could do to Tom, and she *had* done him harm. When she had said she would ruin his character, I had answered, 'You couldn't say a wrong word about him.' And she said, 'I know I couldn't, but lies and mud always stick.' And she was right.

Because Nan really was an ignorant woman, despite her charm. I had lost prestige in the hospital and outside of it because of my association with her. When the matron had said, 'You can't possibly make a friend of her,' I answered, 'If she's good enough to work for me and look after me, then she's good enough to be called friend.' And such was Nan's personality that before very long the matron herself was hobnobbing with her.

But here I was being ordered out by her. The scene that night is imprinted on my mind, for I yelled at her, 'How dare you?' Well, I didn't stop there. Then I dragged open the door and went onto the landing and, for the first time in my life, I exploded in public – and I had plenty of listeners. The boarders were in their rooms, or in the sitting room, stubbing out their cigarettes and spilling their tea and coffee on the lid of my grand piano that Nan had brought down to 'take care of', as I exploded the fallacy of the Diamond Lil. I said things that I never imagined I could say about Sammy, the husband she was ashamed of, and her mentally defective child whom she walked out on in Ireland and then brought over here once she knew my mother was established.

My mother always said caring for the child drove her back to drink because she couldn't stand caring for children that were so handicapped. It was only after one great row that I got Nan to put her into the care of a convent. I yelled out how I had threatened to call in the RSPCC if she beat the child any more, and that this house belonged to me, not her.

Oh, it all came out on that landing, and when I had finished, the house was dead quiet. Then I went into my room, put my outdoor things on and sat on the bed.

It was black outside. There were no buses running to the station. I would have to stay there until the next morning, but I did not lie down.

It was around midnight when she knocked on the door and came in and said she was sorry, and I told her to get out and that as soon as it was light I would leave, and I wanted nothing more to do with her, ever.

And there I sat till five o'clock the following morning when the light was breaking. I thought there was an early workmen's bus that passed down the road about half five. I had two heavy cases and some parcels – the things I was taking back to Hereford with me – and I lined them up on the edge of the pavement and waited. I stood there until quarter past seven in the morning. There was bustle going on in the kitchen: they could see me standing on the pavement, but nobody came out and offered me a drink.

I had the long journey ahead of me to Hereford, and when I reached there I collapsed. What I now know is that with that outburst I had taken a giant step towards the breakdown.

The end of sanity was nearing when I had to make the journey to The Hurst once again: we had let it to a captain and his wife, and she was to take in officers.

My God! Officers. I have spoken about them in *Our Kate*. Even the dirtiest of those poor blind men from London had cleaner habits than those so-called officers.

Tom was with me this time, and we called at the house of one of the schoolmasters. It was blackout when we left, and he led us to the door, bid us a cheery goodbye and closed the door quickly as it was wet. Then there we were outside, and Tom had forgotten the torch. He had also forgotten that there were two flights of stone steps down to the street. He guided me down one set then stepped into the air, pulling me with him. I landed on the pavement on my knees. That was the beginning of phlebitis.

Back in Hereford, I called in the doctor. My knee was swollen, as was the vein from inside the knee to the groin, and I was in acute pain. After his examination, he said, 'Get up out of that bed and move about and busy yourself . . .' I was busying myself at the time eight to ten hours a day sketching cathedrals et cetera for J. Arthur Dixon's Christmas cards. I was cleaning my rooms, cooking Tom a meal at night and writing.

The doctor went out, banging the door behind him. I sat and cried, then got up and followed his advice. Two days passed, and I felt desperately ill. I hobbled to the surgery, where I saw the old doctor. His verdict: 'Get back into bed at once, woman, and stay there. You've got phlebitis, and bad. I'll be round in the morning.'

The following morning, he came and ordered that I had a cage out over my legs and told me that I must keep them as still as possible.

The following day, the young doctor returned. His manner had definitely changed, and he apologised for his rudeness. I imagine he got a ticking off.

Apart from going to the toilet, I hardly moved my body for three weeks. Then one morning something happened: my heart raced and I had a feeling I'd never experienced before. I knew I was going to die. Tom was brought from Madley in a rush; the doctor was brought in too – the old one. After discovering that from when Tom went out in the morning at seven o'clock till he came back at night, I saw no one, and my landscape was the back wall of Bulmer's Cider Factory at the bottom of the small garden, he said I must have a nurse in to see to me and I mustn't get up anymore. He assured me that my heart was all right. He did not tell me that I had had a bout of nervous hysteria.

When the six weeks – or was it seven? – were up, I found I couldn't move my limbs. The doctor thought a week or so in hospital and a change of scene might help me.

I was only in the ward two or three days when the patient opposite, a woman who talked incessantly, informed her visitors, 'That one across there thinks she's bad, but it's just nerves. She's hysterical with them.'

That finished me. From that moment, I entered into a world of fear, hysteria and self-pity.

Nerves? I hadn't nerves. I was ill, but I hadn't nerves. Look at me, all the things I had done off my own bat. Look how I had worked; look how I had got on – a person with nerves couldn't have done that. She couldn't have educated herself like I had, could she? She couldn't have read as widely as I had. A person with nerves couldn't draw or write.

Even today, people go through their life without understanding the effect of the mind on the body. But in 1945, the majority of us were still groping at such knowledge and afraid of it.

I have dealt with my breakdown elsewhere. I will merely say here that the form it took was aggression. I wanted to do something terrible in payment for what had been dealt out to me in my thirty-nine years. My body at the time was very weak. I know now that I had suffered from childhood with anaemia, aggravated by my constant loss of blood from the age of eighteen, and lead poisoning from the two further years I had spent pen painting. I had also, up till then, been troubled by my left leg from the fall in the school yard, and that long stretch of immobility under the cage hadn't helped.

My mind was now a hell filled with hate, fear and a desire for retaliation. I lost all feeling of love; even my feelings for Tom went. I had to tell him so, but being the man he was, he understood. I went voluntarily to a hospital outside of Hereford. I was there for six weeks, and every night that man rode out to see me. It was another seven-mile run from Hereford.

I've also written about my sojourn in the hospital in *Our Kate*. Two months later, I was back in Hastings. Tom had three weeks' compassionate leave, and together with his mother, we set about putting The Hurst in order. Then he had to return to camp.

The war was over but, as Tom said then – and still says – he was a forgotten number, for all his companions and friends in the hut were demobbed, but there he was, still stuck in Madley. It's laughable, but they couldn't find his papers. My prayers had certainly been answered in that direction. But every day now, I was telling God or whoever was there that there was no need to keep him in the air force any longer. Let them find his number and send him home. It was during this waiting that doctors came back into my life once more.

6

As I've said, The Hurst had fifteen rooms, counting the observatory on the fourth floor. It was like a thawing ice box in summer, and in winter it was unbearable. After the war, we were allowed one ton of coal a year, and the only fire we could afford to have was in the study – the smallest of the rooms.

My attire in the winter was somewhere between an Eskimo and a ragman. I was never much good at following a knitting pattern and when I finished the uppers for a pair of woollen boots, I had to get size ten soles to attach them to, then the lining between the knitted uppers and soles used up an entire sheepskin. It took me some time to get used to walking in them but they were so warm, I hated taking them off in exchange for long woollen socks when I got into bed. I also wore combs[4], a vest, knickers, two woollen jumpers and a lined skirt, and over all this an old thick, heavy gentleman's dressing gown – I don't know where I got this garment from. As for my head, it was usually covered by a woollen scarf. I really did look a sight but it was the only way to keep warm, even while sawing up trees outside.

I had worked out a schedule for a twelve-hour day. Three hours were spent trying to get the garden into shape, mostly limbing trees and chopping them up to give me a little warmth at night. I was living alone in this mausoleum during the day, but some friends across the

---

4   An undergarment covering the body and legs.

road in an equally large house did me the *kindness* of allowing me to sleep on the floor in their basement among boxes and rubbish . . . They were very religious people. I repaid them for this *kindness* by helping their sole servant/companion in her tasks, which included washing-up and ironing for a horde of schoolboy boarders.

I was in the continuing depths of the breakdown and fighting fear every minute of the day behind forced laughter.

It was during a session in the garden towards springtime, when I wasn't wearing so many clothes, that I used a pair of long-handled grass-cutting shears to cut a hanging limb from a tree. I lifted them at arm's length and with a great effort brought them crashing together on the branch, which turned out to be rotten. The two handles hit the sides of my breasts with such force that, when I later picked myself up from the ground, I imagined for a moment that another time bomb had gone off quite near.

I watched my flat bosom expand daily – I was as thin as two plates – and I wrote to my mother-in-law telling her what I had done and how ill I felt because of it. She came down unexpectedly from Grays [in Essex] and found me lying on the palette on the floor in the basement of my kind friends' house. She couldn't believe that anyone could treat me so. She got me up and over to our house and went to call the doctor, but I stopped her. I would go and see him. I had learned that if you were unfortunate enough to have had a breakdown, every following ailment was imaginary. I had already come face to face with this particular doctor – I didn't like him, and he didn't like me.

We had been acquainted from when I first went to Hastings in 1930, and he wasn't used to young women of twenty-four, and *single*, asking him for an examination in order that she could put another £250 on an already £500 insurance.

'Why are you putting so much money into insurance? Thinking about committing suicide?'

'Not at present,' I had answered. What I didn't say was, 'I'm saving to provide myself with a good home for I can't see me marrying a man who will provide me with what I want.' I was very much out of love in those days and I never thought I would love again.

'There's a lien on the policy – why?' he said.

'It's a family matter,' I said. Why hadn't I the courage to tell him I was a bastard? Facing up to it then might have saved me a lot of trouble later on.

However, here I was, standing in front of him.

'Hello. What's wrong now?'

You'd think I'd been to him every week; I'd only seen him twice in the past six months.

'It's my breasts, doctor – they're swollen.'

He looked from one to the other, then said, 'Yes, yes, they do seem a bit high. How did that come about?'

I told him, giving both a verbal and active description because at first he couldn't understand how I had been so stupid as to hit both my breasts with a pair of shears. I had to convince him that shears came in different sizes.

A short time later, he came out from behind the screen saying, 'Get your things on.' Then as he washed his hands he shouted, 'It isn't cancer.'

I never thought it was cancer; you didn't get cancer by hitting yourself with the handles of grass edgers.

'It's mastitis.'

'Wh–at?'

'I said, it's mastitis.'

I appeared at the edge of the screen and I said again, 'Wh–at?'

Drying his hands, he looked at me and slowly said, 'You have the unfortunate habit, Mrs Cookson, of answering and prefixing all statements with wh–at. I find this very irritating.'

'*Well, what is mastitis?*' I demanded.

'It's what you've got. Lumps on the breasts. Cows get it in their udders.'

'Co–ws?'

'Yes, I said cows. It stops them giving milk. But that won't affect you.'

Going to his desk he said, 'I'll give you a prescription for a camp brassiere.'

'Wh—?'

'Yes, you want to know what a camp brassiere is. Well, it's a bras-siere, only stronger and bigger and' – he demonstrated with two spread hands over his chest – 'it's firm-like; it supports the breasts. Anyway,' he added, 'you could say you've got one over on the cows in this instance.'

Standing silently looking down on him, I saw passing over him a herd of cows and me in the middle of them on all fours. We were all wearing camp brassieres; the only difference between us was that my udders seemed to be swinging in a different direction from theirs.

'What are you smiling about?'

I tried to tell him, but it didn't sound funny in the telling, and he didn't laugh. He handed me the prescription and I went out, feeling deflated, as I was to feel every time I left his surgery in the years that followed.

They found Tom's number, and he came home. I remember that day as I stood in his arms with the tears washing my face. I thought, 'If I don't get better now, I never will.' I didn't know it was going to take ten or more years to clear my head of that breakdown, and that weeks, even months, would pass before I would know part of a day free from fear.

Tom was fighting a battle of his own, too. He was always reticent about how he felt. It was many years later when he opened up and told me his reactions to the five years he had spent in the RAF, when he had realised the other men weren't superior to him because he was only five foot five and had risen from the working class. He had realised, too, that he had a mind that was superior to the majority of men he came across. He was, in one way, fortunate that his close associates in Madley had been men like Joe Raine, Joe Golding and Reg Greatorex. But when they were posted towards the end of the war, he came up against the rough and tumble, and the main topics of conversation were how many times they could have it off with this one or that one, and getting away with stealing, wheeling and dealing.

I would not have Tom take anything during the war that did not belong to him, but once a fortnight, when on night duty, he was given rations. He would take them back the next morning – they must have thought him mad.

I thought this was going too far the other way. 'They're your due,' I used to say. Yet I admired him for his restraint. He even went for his own mother when the whole family came on holiday after the war and she brought a store of black-market butter et cetera. He would not eat any of it. Oh, I remember the rumpus that caused. That visit wasn't a happy one. Strangely, I got the blame for making their Tom like that.

When Tom returned to teach at the school, there was no resemblance to the timid young master that had been evacuated with the boys six years previously.

He threw himself into activities: football, cricket, scouting, common-room meetings et cetera, et cetera. This meant that, apart from his presence at meals, I was alone in the house most days – not only during the week, but at weekends and many evenings too. There was a great aloneness in me, and I said to him, 'I would like a dog for company.'

'Yes, yes, all right, we'll have a dog.'

One of the masters was looking after a bull terrier for a friend and his wife, who were on holiday. The dog was the runt of the litter, and the master had been asked to find a home for it if possible.

Well, the first time I saw Bill, he bounced towards me and I literally bounced towards him and hugged him. He was mine.

We took him home, but encountered a problem: we couldn't get him to go out of the gate for a walk – he was terrified to leave the grounds. I found out he had been passed on from this one to that one, and now he thought a gate meant he was going to be pushed out once more. Slowly, we convinced him that he was ours.

Bill may have been ungainly and ugly, but to me he was beautiful. I'd had him for three weeks when one day there was a knock at the front door and there was a lady . . . Did I say lady? Well, we'll give her that title for the time being.

'You have my dog,' she said.

'Your dog?'

'Yes, the bull terrier . . . Do you want to keep him?'

'Yes, yes, of course. Come in.'

Bill recognised the lady straightaway and went to hide under the table. She said again, 'So you intend to keep him?'

'Yes, yes. I understood that the owner was looking for a home for him.'

'Oh, that's nonsense. He has a pedigree, and I'm the owner. He is for sale; his price is ten pounds.'

'*Wh–at?*'

Believe it or not, Tom and I hadn't ten pounds between us at the time. We had used the money I'd saved up over the years – stupidly, I realised now – to pay off all the mortgage on The Hurst, which came to over £500, because we didn't want to be in debt in any way.

'I understood he was the runt of the litter.'

'Nonsense. I breed pedigrees, not runts. Well, do you want it?' said the genteel lady.

I got on my hind legs. 'I'm not paying ten pounds for the dog. It was given to me.'

'That person had no right to give it away; it wasn't his. He had instructions to sell it.'

The person was a schoolmaster and a friend of Tom's.

'Well?'

'I'm not paying ten pounds, thank you.'

She looked about her.

Flanking the stone fireplace, I had some highly polished brass and copper articles, including a big hot water can that the servants at one time had to carry from the kitchen to the far-away bedrooms for the ladies' and gentlemen's baths – even at this stage of my life, I can feel anger at what servants were subjected to in the big houses. Underneath it, there was a large plate-warming stand with a place for a burner – quite an antique piece. There was also a large copper bowl with a lid – I have never found out what use this was put to – and various other pieces.

'Those are nice,' she said. 'I tell you what, I'll take them in place of the dog.'

My brass and copper that I polished every week, that lit up the grey stone of the fireplace and the panelling of the hall? Never. I forgot about my feelings for Bill. 'Take him,' I said.

The dog cringed when she went to pick him up. I followed her to the door and watched her throw him into the back of the car. He immediately looked out of the back window. I followed the car to the gate and there he was, howling at me. She slowly started her journey down the road. All of a sudden, I was bounding after her. 'Give him here,' I cried. 'You can have the brass.'

Almost gleefully, she returned and whipped up one thing after another from the hearth.

Tom couldn't believe what was happening and on his return to school he told the master in question, who didn't believe it either.

The next morning, a private car came to the door and the driver handed me all my pieces of brass and copper, and by the next post I received a letter from the lady's husband apologising profusely for my experience.

He was a solicitor . . . She was a bitch.

When I took Bill for his injection later, the vet said he was a poor specimen: his legs were too short and slightly bandy and his head was too big. Why did I buy a dog like that, he asked?

◆ ◆ ◆

I've described elsewhere how, when we escaped from the vet's, Bill took me at a run down London Road onto the front and we did a marathon along half of the Hastings promenade, which is over two miles long . . .

Then came the day when his hair began to fall out and left big spotty patches all over his body, which he scratched until they bled. We couldn't afford a vet's bill, so I took him to the PDSA. They didn't say what was wrong with him, but they gave me a big bottle of clear liquid to apply to the sores. That poor dog nearly went up the wall every time he saw that bottle. I didn't know until later that it was pure carbolic I was patting into his sores.

Needless to say, still in the breakdown, I was feeling awful. To add to this, I had started an early menopause – that was all I needed to be getting on with, but I had to have a little more.

The spots appeared on my head and brow at first. I couldn't stand the irritation, so there I was, facing my doctor again. *My*, did I say? I didn't want him any more than he wanted me. I should merely have said, the doctor.

'What's the matter now?'

'I'm coming out in spots, doctor.'

'Where?'

'On my head, and look, on my brow.'

With a stub end of a pencil, he moved my hair here and there.

'You've got dandruff,' he said.

I nearly hit the roof. 'I've never had dandruff in my life. I wash my hair every week.'

'You've got dandruff, woman. If you wash it every week, do it from now on with an anti-dandruff soap. Good morning.'

The following week, I was covered from head to toe with these spots. I was as demented as the dog, but I let another week go by before I ventured into the surgery again.

He looked up at me. 'My God! What's happened to you this time?'

'I don't know. I'm covered all over.'

He was gingerly poking at me while tut-tutting, 'Been abroad?'

'*No.*'

'Been mixing with foreigners?'

'No, I haven't been mixing with foreigners.'

'Well, where have you been to get this?'

'I don't know, you tell me. I've spent the last three weeks looking after my dog; he's got mange.'

'*Oh my God!*' He backed from me, then shook his head before he said, 'One in a million human beings gets mange and you'd have to be that one, wouldn't you.'

He now started taking tomes down from a shelf and flicking through their pages. When he found what he wanted, he said two words.

'Sheep dip.' He looked up at me.

'Wh–at?'

'It's just another name for it. That's the only thing that'll cure it.'

'*Sheep dip?*'

'Yes. What they push the sheep through to clear them of ticks.'

I had a vivid mental picture of a trough bordered on each side by grinning yokels, and there was I, starkers, being prodded through the dip.

It didn't appear funny.

He was writing at his desk now. 'Take this to the chemist, but before you go in you'd better buy yourself a three- or four-inch distemper brush.'

'Wh–at? I mean, why do I want a distemper brush?'

'Because it will be easier to apply this stuff with. Get your husband to do it, and you must see that he brushes it all over you . . . No little parts missing, mind, and don't wear any clothes for the next three days, just a light wrap, then have a bath and if the stuff's done its work, you'll be clear. If not, you'll have to start all over again.' He was trying to suppress a smile.

How I hated that man.

It was the depths of winter, we only had that tiny fire in the study, as I said, and it could have been a candle on my bare pelt as Tom, according to instructions, painted me all over.

Apart from diving out of that room through the icy corridor and upstairs into the lavatory, I stayed there for the three days, then had a bath and, as . . . that man . . . had prophesied, the sheep dip did the trick.

Well, if it did it for me, it would do it for Bill. I got another huge bottle of the stuff, bathed Bill in it, and Tom ran him around the lawn for half an hour so that it would dry into him and he wouldn't lick it off.

Bill too was cured.

We had Bill for nine years, and there was hardly a day that went by that he didn't cause us some worry because he loved people and hated dogs. There were times when Tom had to beat him with a stick to prise his mouth open to release some poor animal that he had gone for. This aggression began when he was two years old, when his pal from next door, a Labrador, came into our garden and buried his bone. Bill sniffed at the hole and decided to investigate, whereupon the Labrador returned and sprung on him. Bill, who had never had a fight before that, was almost torn to pieces. From that time, he would never let a dog near him. We sought advice from the vet. He said there were two kinds of aggressiveness: one protective, the other a fighting one. He could spay him, and if he was of the protective kind he would become quieter, but he could do nothing about the other kind.

The climax came when some children arrived at the door with a dog. Fortunately, Bill was in the kitchen. What would have happened otherwise might have been disastrous for the children. So, reluctantly, we decide that he must be put to sleep.

The vet said that after he spayed him we could finally make up our minds whether he should wake him or let him go on sleeping permanently.

The morning the vet was due to take him away, I couldn't bear it; I had to go out. I said goodbye to him. What followed was uncanny. The vet was supposed to come at twelve o'clock, but when I returned home at one, the vet hadn't come. Bill, who always bounded towards me when I entered the gate, was sitting in the yard pressed close to the wall, his face turned from me. I passed him and he didn't move. It was a weird experience; he knew what was before him.

The vet could hardly have got him into the surgery when I phoned and said, it didn't matter what happened – I wanted him back. He came back the next day and he must have been in pain, but so gentle was his nature with everything except dogs that he allowed Tigger the cat to curl up between his legs in his basket. She was very fond of him, and Tigger lived until she was twenty-one.

I've written about Bill's death in *Hamilton*. I couldn't write about it again; it is too painful.

7

As part of her recovery following her breakdown, Catherine started writing in 1945. She joined the Hastings Writers' Group, where she read her work aloud. In 1950, Catherine's first novel, Kate Hannigan, *was published, followed by* The Fifteen Streets: *both sold out of their initial printings. Her nineteenth novel,* Katie Mulholland *(published in 1967), was largely considered her breakthrough bestseller, but she would go on to write more than 100 books, largely inspired by her childhood in the north-east, selling more than 100 million copies across the world.*

In 1947, Tom went to his first big scout camp in Wales, and I went with him.

Why did I do it, when I knew it was frowned upon by the masters? No wife accompanied her husband to a scout camp; it had never been heard of. Why did I put Tom in this awkward position? Well, it was the lesser of two evils for both of us. We neither of us wanted to be parted for a fortnight; we were made that way right from the beginning. If I didn't go with him, I would be left alone in that big house on my own and, I hate to keep pressing the point, I was bleeding at both ends.

I understand that ten per cent of women can go through the menopause and not even recognise there's any change in their body. Another thirty per cent can have a slight difficulty – hot flushes et cetera. Another thirty percent can have it bad. This last thirty can go through hell. In this section, the mind can become affected. Here you have the breakdowns and the nerve cases. I was still in mine, but the menopause gave it depth and height. I asked the question that tens of thousands of women have asked before me: Why should I have to go through this? It is of little consolation to know now that men experience the menopause too, though it takes them in different ways – as bits on the side and divorce courts prove.

I had put in some practice of sleeping out in preparation for the camp. In fact, Tom and I often used to sleep on the lawn, and people seeing us imagined that the house was full of guests. Guests were the last things we wanted to see; we wanted no one but each other.

Anyway, there I was, laden down with kit at the tail end of sixty scouts holding up the traffic in a London thoroughfare on our way to the station and deep Wales. My presence elicited a remark from a passerby, 'Look at that daisy mixed up with the scouts.' And I must have looked a daisy.

It was an awful journey through the night. We arrived next morning in the Welsh countryside. The rain was pelting down, and we had an almost two-mile tramp to the camp. We reached a little farmhouse that could have been dug out of the seventeenth century. A gulley ran down in front of the cottage and the cow byres, taking away the slush. When I enquired if I could use their toilet, I caused embarrassment. It turned out to be bushes in the summer – what it was in the winter, I did not enquire.

The scout tents were pitched in a valley at the head of a cove. I was isolated in a field on a hill overlooking them. It was full of cows. It was my first acquaintance with the animals at close range, and I was petrified of them, even when I imagined them with camp brassieres on. Nevertheless, I pitched my tent and got my fire going and my little tin kettle boiling, to the amazement of groups of scouts searching hopelessly for bits of dry kindling.

When news reached the camp that Mrs Cookson had a fire going, Tom came bounding up, pride oozing out of him.

'How on earth did you manage that, dear?'

'I brought a bundle of firelighters with me.'

'*Never*. It isn't done, dear.'

'It's done now. I'm no scout . . . Would you like a cup of tea?'

I am sensitive to places, and I didn't like the cove where the scouts had a campfire on the second evening. I didn't join in the singing – I had a shivery feeling. Thinking it was just my imagination, I made my way down there the following day, but had the urge to scuttle away from it. Why? I couldn't explain. 'Don't be silly,' I told myself. 'It's likely just because the bay's enclosed by cliffs on two sides.'

Towards the end of our stay, I was in the farm kitchen getting some milk, when the farmer's wife asked if I had enjoyed the camp. The farmer, his son and daughter were in the kitchen too, and when my answer was not immediately forthcoming, they all looked at me. Trying not to hurt their feelings, I said I wasn't very fond of the bay, but I couldn't explain why. I recall that they gazed at each other, and then there was a silence and I felt I had upset them.

When I left, the daughter followed me outside and said, 'You know that's strange, very strange, about you not liking the bay. You see, I had another brother; he and' – she mentioned the name of her present brother – 'used to go swimming often in the bay, and one morning they went out and all of a sudden my brother went straight down, just like that.'

If I remember rightly, his body was never recovered, but it gave me the shivers, for I had sensed something dreadful had happened in that bay and I've had a number of experiences with regard to the bad or evil things that have occurred in different places.

During the many camps I followed over the years, most of my time was spent lying in my tent – which was now a large one – painting or writing, for I cannot remember any one camp where I was not bleeding: either from the menopause or my nose or tongue or finger tips, and often it was a combined operation. I have learned since that some of the inner bleeding was from the telangiectases.

At one period, I went to the doctor again. 'How long does the menopause last?' I asked him. 'Oh, two years at the most,' he said. I had then been in it for four and it was still going strong. Twice, I'd been in hospital for scraping.

Then came a time when for weeks on end the bleeding never stopped, day after day, until I could hardly walk. I think of it as my eleven-week period, and during this time I spent a fortnight under canvas; literally staying there. We were down in Somerset, and the camp broke up just the day before the great flood. Tom had wanted me to stay on at a hotel and have a rest. All I wanted was to get home – and it was lucky I did.

Then came the night I was playing bridge at the headmaster's house when I felt something go click inside – it was just like the warnings I got before the miscarriages.

We hadn't a car at the time. Two bus rides and half a mile tramp up the road later, I collapsed into bed. It was nine o'clock; by twelve the place was a shambles. In desperation, Tom phoned the doctor.

This doctor had a rather beautiful wife. She looked so delicate, fragile even, that it was impossible to believe that she could swear like a trooper. She was in bed with her husband, and she greeted Tom's desperate call by saying, 'It's the bloody Cookson woman; she's bleeding.'

He came on the phone, and what he said to Tom was, 'Stick some blocks under the bed.'

Believe it or not, that's what he said. Because don't forget, I'd had a breakdown, hence everything was imagination coupled with exaggeration.

Tom couldn't stick blocks under the bed, but he put pillows under my legs.

By six o'clock the next morning, I wasn't aware of very much, but I learned he had phoned my friend who was the wife of another maths master; she had had experience of operations. They both came immediately. The result was she spoke to the doctor and he was in the house in a very short time, and by eight o'clock I was in hospital in Fredrick Road – the same place I'd worked in for ten years up to the war.

This was on a Thursday morning. A young medic saw me as the doctor had gone to a conference or some such and wouldn't be back till Monday. And there I lay, my nerves in such a jangle I wanted to scream, for opposite me was one of those loud-voiced 'I'm the kind of patient that gets on with everybody. I joke with the doctors and the nurses. I call up the ward to the far end and have a conversation with Mrs X. I tell everybody about my many operations and I diagnose others and tell them what they're in for' women. She talked fourteen hours of the twenty-four – she was an old hand. I thought I would go mad. Really mad.

On the Saturday night, there was a picture show and the apparatus was placed at the bottom of my bed.

On the Monday, at three o'clock in the afternoon, the doctor came to see me.

'Hello, my dear, what's all this?'

By this time, I wasn't aware of much, only that it was taking every bit of energy that I ever had just to stay awake.

I was past explaining, so I let him find out for himself. And he did, and what he said was, 'Good Lord! It's a whopping great polypus. Have you been bleeding like this long?'

'Only eleven weeks or so,' I managed to say with as much sarcasm as I could muster.

There was an exchange of glances across the bed. I was bundled onto a stretcher into a lift and up into the theatre where, once again, they were still clearing the gore from the last do.

It's impossible to believe now that of the numerous operations I'd had, I had never once been given a pre-med sedative. Mostly, I was pushed into a theatre, as on this occasion, when they were clearing up the fore. I saw them take my legs one after the other and thrust them into straps, hoist them up then pull me down towards the edge of the table and place a bucket there. When one of them stuck a needle in my arm, he exclaimed, 'Oh, God! It's broken.'

In the pause that followed I remember clearly thinking, 'I'll not die from the operation; I'll die from my heart stopping dead with fear.'

The arch light was blinding me, a needle went in again and a voice said, 'Begin counting.'

When I got to past twenty there were murmurs of, 'Good Lord! Well, well!' The last I heard was, 'She decided not to go off.'

When I returned home a week later, I lay in that dim little study at my very lowest ebb. Tom used to dash home at dinner time and make me a meal, and I never saw anyone again until he finished school. I felt so weak and ill that I was tempted again and again to just let go and die. When three days had gone by and I could hardly eat or sleep, Tom phoned the doctor and asked if he would please call. His response was to send a pamphlet on remedial recuperation. It gave instructions on the pastimes you could take to help yourself, such as knitting et cetera.

I recall how I cried that day, and I called out to God and asked why I was being treated so. Was it because I had denied him? And I answered myself emphatically, 'No, no. If this was the work of a God, then He was the essence of a spiteful, mean power and I wanted nothing to do with him. I would rely on myself, yes I would.'

But it was a very depleted self, for I didn't know then how anaemic I was; how in need of iron I was; how low my blood count was . . . Blood test? I'd never had a blood test.

If a reader ever gets this far – and I doubt it – but if they do, they will think, 'The whole blooming thing is about the awful doctors she's had and how ill she's been et cetera.'

Yes, that is right. That's what it's all about because that has been my life – how I feel, how my illnesses have made me feel, and the struggle against them. Oh, yes, you're quite right, the whole thing is about illness and doctors and jealousy and evil, but I'll come to that.

It's hard for me to realise now that, in spite of everything happening, I was still writing. I had joined a writers' circle, where I read my Mary Ann stories aloud, and I felt so grateful to those who said they liked them.

Through the writing of these stories, I was trying to erase the pity that had erupted in me for this poor child who had gone through so much. I was trying to recall that I had laughed and that there were certain things I had enjoyed before the breakdown. But it's hard trying to dig up humour when you are still riddled with fear and aggressiveness. About this time, during one of my clever-clog periods, I remember stating that humour was the poor cousin of wit and at best it was the whetstone on which wit sharpened itself – that one laughs at humour but savours wit. Yet I've never succeeded at wit and am, I should say, content to plump for humour and laughter, which, it is amazing to recall, I still managed to raise when in company.

CATHERINE COOKSON AS A CHILD (BORN 27TH JUNE 1906)

From the Catherine Cookson Collection, Howard Gottlieb Archival Research Centre at Boston University

CATHERINE COOKSON'S THOUGHTS ON REJECTION

All my pals were going to the party so I was going to the party. And I asked Kate for a new hair ribbon, I remember, and she said to me: don't you want to go to the Crown, hinnie? The Crown was a picture house in Tyne dock. I always went there on a Saturday, but no, I knew I wanted a clean pinnie on with my hair ribbon because I was going to that party.

Down that back lane, I saw all the girls going into this back door. I hadn't been invited to the party. But I knew that I had to get into that party.

And I stood outside. The back door was closed but I thought that Mrs [Blank] didn't know that I was waiting to get into the party and if I jumped up and down, she would come to the window. Somebody came to the window but nobody invited me to the party. But I had to get into that party. I gatecrashed through the back door. There was upstairs and downstairs and they lived upstairs. So I knocked on the staircase door – and I could see this girl coming down the stairs. There was a sort of a confab at the stair head and this little girl came down the stairs. And you know, children are cruel – they don't intend to be, it's their nature, all children are cruel – but she just repeated what her mother or father had said, and she said, 'Y'cannae' come t'me party because you haven't got no da.'

And I think the new buildings in East Jarrow changed from that day for me. I felt that I was rejected. I knew before that I hadn't got no da but from that day on, life changed and I was going to show them, by God I was going to show them. Even as a child, because from that day I started – no, it was from the day I knew she told me I hadn't a da that I started to fight. From that day I became aggressive.

I remember Kate knew what was going to happen; she knew I wouldn't get into that party, and she said to me, 'Never you mind, hinnie. You'll have your day with them.'

And Kate, I have.

'MY MOTHER, WHO WAS ABOUT TWENTY-TWO AT THE TIME,
I THINK.'

From the Catherine Cookson Collection, Howard Gottlieb Archival
Research Centre at Boston University

CATHERINE COOKSON'S THOUGHTS ON POVERTY

But it was our family, our lot, that if they hadn't drunk, we wouldn't have been as poor as we were. The only happy times that I really had in my young days was when we were poor – when we had nothing and there was no money for beer, just enough for the bare necessities of food.

Those were the happy times that I had.

'HOW I LOOKED DURING THE PERIOD 1937–40 WHEN I
RARELY SMILED: A BITTER PERIOD.'

From the Catherine Cookson Collection, Howard Gottlieb Archival
Research Centre at Boston University

CATHERINE COOKSON'S THOUGHTS ON HER NERVOUS BREAKDOWN

If you present me with a choice of a malignant disease and a breakdown, I can tell you which I would take – the disease anytime! I wasn't only absolutely fearing – I became aggressive! Of all the things I've gone through, I wanted to hit back at all the people who had caused it and mostly Kate and, as I say in my book, I felt like killing her.

◆ ◆ ◆

To describe a breakdown is beyond me. I can only say that I lived with this fear that made me sick. That I couldn't sleep.

I always wanted to be fifty. If I was fifty, I thought things and life would become easy. And it was strange – for when I was fifty, things did change.

◆ ◆ ◆

At the beginning and the end it is you who has got to fight this thing. To face up to it in yourself. You've got to use a breakdown as a mirror and you've got to see, you've got to go back and find out what's brought you to this state, which I did. You have to see yourself as you were and I saw I had been living a false life.

I have been living behind a facade for years.

'ST HELEN'S WORKHOUSE, HASTINGS, 1935. PICNIC FOR
THE INMATES.'

From the Catherine Cookson Collection, Howard Gottlieb Archival
Research Centre at Boston University

'MY SELF-IMPROVEMENT — FENCING DAYS.'

From the Catherine Cookson Collection, Howard Gottlieb Archival
Research Centre at Boston University

'WE WERE MARRIED IN JUNE 1940.'

From the Catherine Cookson Collection, Howard Gottlieb Archival
Research Centre at Boston University

TOM COOKSON ON
CATHERINE'S WRITING

If you want to review her books, you can skim through them like lightning and you'd say, by, that's a jolly good story and there's nothing in it. Ah! But that's where you're wrong. If you then sit down and read it, you will find all the wisdom of the world! Everybody is in that book: you, I, and that person reading it.

'MY MOTHER, 1935.'
KATE IN HER FIFTIES.

From the Catherine Cookson Collection, Howard Gottlieb Archival
Research Centre at Boston University

CATHERINE COOKSON'S THOUGHTS ON PEACE OF MIND

I couldn't get it out of my system until my mother died. And I brought her from the north here to Hastings. She was dying then but I knew that she had to go on living because I had to get rid of this hate I had for her. I had to have my chance as well as she had to have her chance and so I looked after her for three years and it was the happiest three years I ever had with her. I mourned her when she died, very much. But then I knew that my release was coming and I must write it out of my system. And so I say here:

I have written my tale in the room where Kate died. The roses are tapping on the window again and her presence is strong about me. I look towards the corner where her bed stood and she is smiling at me.

'You'll feel better now, lass.'

'You think so?'

'I'm sure of it.'

'I've tried to be fair.'

'You were always fair, lass, always. And you haven't put down half that happened. You never need to worry about not being fair, but because you've learned to forgive things will settle in you now.'

And I think that was the point: I'd learned to forgive. And from then things have settled in me. And I now know peace of mind to such an extent that I never thought possible.

'SHIPMATES! HAPPY TIMES.'
THE BOAT IS NAME AFTER THE MARY ANN SHAUGHNESSY

From the Catherine Cookson Collection, Howard Gottlieb Archival
Research Centre at Boston University

8

Catherine and Tom lived at The Hurst, on and off, until 1954, when they moved to a house called Loreto, also in Hastings. Catherine had moved Kate in with them the previous year, as her mother was unwell; in 1956 she died of stomach cancer. After Kate's death, Catherine began to write her first autobiography: it would take her twelve years and eight rewrites, but in 1969 Our Kate was published. The same year, Tom took early retirement on grounds of his health; he would continue to support and care for Catherine for the rest of their lives.

It was during the 1940s that I longed to be fifty; once I was fifty, I thought everything would settle in me and I would somehow start a new life. And I did, but not in the way I expected. What I was really asking for was peace of mind: relief from fear, and goodbye to the menopause and, of course, the breakdown.

From the time I returned home in 1945 until the end of 1946, I was writing plays and short stories and articles. The latter two I frequently sent away, but without success. I carried out my writing between keeping that giant house clean, working in the garden, shopping in the town – which was two miles away and the nearest bus stop over half a mile distance – cooking and mending. And when I say mending, I mean mending: darning Tom's socks and sewing up ladders in my artificial silk stockings, remaking my own clothes and, of course, making hats. I loved hats. I had a passion for hats. I had a big black straw that I used to trim up.

All the masters' wives came out in their best for sports day and commemoration day and suchlike. One particular day, I wanted a new hat, so I covered this big black shape with a large black veil edged with silk pom-poms. It was very striking. At least I thought so, until one of the masters laughingly said, 'I like the antimacassar on your hat, Kitty.'

I had a taste for dresses in those days too, and a weakness for veils.

Up to this time, I had never tried to write a novel. The characters in the plays were always middle class or from the upper strata in the style of Lord Chesterfield, but for a long time my mind had been nagging at me, telling me they weren't real. 'Write about the people you know. Remember what Kate used to tell you about her early days, and those of her mother, and have a go at that.'

I had a go. It was after I'd written three chapters that I went to hear Christopher Bush give a talk in the Hastings Library. The title was, 'How to Write a Novel'. This is something else I've explained elsewhere: how I became so annoyed when he said anybody who could write a laundry list could write a novel, and I tackled him with it. The outcome was that he gave me the address of his agent and told me to send what work I'd done to him. This was how I became acquainted with a John Smith of the agency Christy and Moore, Gerrards Cross. This man wrote straight back to me and told me to get the story finished and let him have it. I did just that – although it took me a year.

John Smith sent the book to Macdonalds, where Murray Thompson read the first chapter, then said to his secretary, 'Send it back. It's too grim.' What she did was take it home and read the book that night. The next morning, she said to him, 'I think you've missed something here.' And that was the beginning.

What ecstasy, what glory. I was a writer. Everybody would rejoice with me. Now they would know I wasn't just somebody who had been manageress of a workhouse laundry and had gatecrashed into the precincts of the holy grammar school circle. They would know I had talent. I somehow felt that they should have realised this from my drawings, but as one person had said to me: 'Anybody can draw with a little effort; it's the first thing a child does after prattling.'

The acceptance of my book was to open my eyes to a side of human nature I hadn't yet encountered: jealousy. I could never imagine anyone being jealous.

◆　◆　◆

There was a clique of wives in the grammar school with three leaders; they were joined by one or two outsiders and were all interested in Dr Barnado's and worked for the bazaars. I was in the group but not of it. We had meetings in our respective houses once a month. When I joyfully joined the meeting just after it had become known that my book was to be published, not one of these so-called ladies made any reference to it, nor to the fact that that week I had been fortunate enough to be on *Woman's Hour*. It was my first talk. Of course, I was in a way prepared for this reaction, as the leader of the gang was our closest neighbour. She is dead now, so I am not hurting her when I say that she was not only spiteful but wicked in her reactions towards me.

Trying to keep on the best side of her, the night I returned from London after doing a voice test at the BBC, and knowing that I was to go on the radio, Tom said to me, 'I think you'd better go and tell her.' She had been a member of the same writers' circle as me, but she couldn't stand the acclaim I received for my Mary Ann stories, so she ceased to attend. On this evening, I went through her gate – her husband was feeding the chickens on the lawn as they were great naturalists. I knocked on the open kitchen door and she came to it, smiling her false smile, remarking that I was all dressed up and where had I been? Like a fool, I always deprecated myself to her and the rest of the gang, wanting so much to be liked and accepted. And so I said, 'You wouldn't believe it. I can't believe it myself; they must be short of talent. I've been up in London to the BBC. I wrote an article . . . I'm going on next month.' I remember I kept nodding my head like an idiot.

I saw her expression change. There was a silence between us, then taking the door in her hand she banged it in my face. Her husband kept his head down as I passed him on my way out.

I literally staggered out of that garden, through our gate, over the drive and into the house, and I couldn't see where I was going, for all the tears were blinding me.

That crowd caused me many anguished tears.

My neighbour's next reaction to my success was to head a number of protests in order to get my book banned. It's laughable when I think of it, yet sad to think to what lengths jealousy can drive a highly intelligent woman; a woman with a university degree – something that I, from my lowly station, saw as the pinnacle of success, but which apparently did nothing for her.

The housekeeper in the house across the road was a staunch disciple of the protesters. She stated in public that decent people should object to my story because of what I had written in the first few pages. Believe it or not, I had described a baby being brought into the world by a young doctor, and the child was covered with a caul. That was their main objection. Of course, it was banned in Ireland because of my opinion of the Catholic Church, but this wasn't Ireland – this was Hastings, England.

But there were bright spots in my first efforts. Many of the masters' wives were very nice people. This was made apparent when they only appeared at functions once or twice a year and didn't join the gang. What pleased me more than anything was that the English master, Mr Connesby, who was held in very high esteem, wrote me a beautiful letter praising the book.

John Betjeman praised the book too, among others. So I was away.

It was at this time in 1950 that Nan Smith came onto my horizon again. I hadn't seen her since our fracas at the beginning of 1946 when she wanted to sell Elphinstone Mount.

I had, before the war, and immediately after buying Elphinstone Mount, sold a piece of adjoining land for £500 but, on agreement, had to pay £200 straightaway to the building society. The other £300 I had handed over to Nan because she was just starting out on her own. Looking back, I must have been barmy because I had hardly a penny myself.

That morning in 1946, there she was in the solicitor's office saying that she wanted to sell the house and the solicitor telling her that the house was not hers to sell. The only way she could acquire the house was by deed of gift from me.

Tom, wanting her out of my life altogether, had said, 'Let her have the lot.'

I said, 'No way.' I had kept that house going for the first two years of the war for her and I'd had to pay off her debts. She had made money hand over fist from the boarders during the war years. Where had it gone? Because she said she had nothing now. She also said she had had an offer of £1000 for the house but there was still a debt of a few hundred to pay off. I said I would halve the profit with her. She wasn't having that; no, not at all. She offered me £250. I walked out. Tom was outside and sent me back again, saying, 'Let her have the lot. Get rid of her.'

Reluctantly, I settled for the £250.

It was a few weeks later when I received a letter from a builder asking when I was going to settle the bill for the work he had done in order to sell the house. He went on to say – in so many words – that he didn't think he should have had any need to ask me to settle when I'd got over £4000 for it. I couldn't believe it. But yes, that's what she had got. I was enraged. When I tackled her with it, she dared to say she had earned it for the work she had done from when she had met me all those years ago in the laundry.

Her wage had never been more than thirty shillings a week even when she became attendant in the house part of the Institution, and out of the pound she paid me she had to be kept, as had her daughter. She was a chain-smoker, going through twenty or thirty cigarettes a day, and always the best brand, besides which she did her betting pool and horses.

More than once, Tom had tactfully pointed out to me that I was being robbed, but I wouldn't believe him. Good old Nan wouldn't steal from me.

Tom said now, 'Forget it, that's the finish. You're clear of her.'

But here she was on this summer day in 1950. Eight years since I had finally broken with her, and four years since the Elphinstone affair. She looked different – pale and drawn – but her manner was quite airy. She had heard that I had had a book published and had come to congratulate me, but didn't she know right from the beginning that I would make it in the literary world, because hadn't she read all my bits and pieces over the years? She would have been up sooner to congratulate me, but she had been in Ireland and she hadn't been well; she'd been in hospital.

My reception of her was stiff.

Some months later, a neighbour asked whether I had heard Nan Smith had been made bankrupt.

I couldn't believe it, because with the money she had made out of Elphinstone Mount, she had bought a great big house in its own grounds, then sold it to the Church of England nuns for quite a large sum. She had also bought war-damaged property all over the town and had let flats – and this had been her downfall. First, she had been taken to court for overcharging rent, then the man who was working for her to fix the war-damaged properties had been unable to get his money and so had made her bankrupt. She had an overdraft of £80,000.

Three incidents had happened between the time she had visited me and when she was finally declared bankrupt. The first was to do with the morning I received a letter from the manager of the Westminster Bank to say that I was two pounds overdrawn and what was I going to do about it?

I had been with this bank since I had first come to Hastings in 1930. Tom's cheque went in every month; we didn't owe anyone a penny. How had I come to be two pounds overdrawn? I went down to the bank manager.

I recall he pointed out that the bank didn't make mistakes. Yes, of course he got my husband's cheque every month, but it was well to point out that one should look to one's expenditure. Then he said something that almost caused his early demise. 'You were once employed by Mrs Smith, weren't you?'

They heard my voice in every corner of that bank. '*How dare you, and how dare she?*' I gave him the history before stamping out. It was clear that Nan Smith had taken money from my account as if it was hers.

It was many, many years later, when I had become a name and my bank balance was very warm, that I made an appointment to see the then bank manager and went to the counter where you rang the bell for service.

In line with my eye were two clerks who were busy chatting and took no notice of my presence. I rang the bell again. One glanced towards me, then went on talking. My third ringing of the bell caught the attention of a woman clerk further down the room. This clerk indicated that there was someone at the window; they indicated in turn that she could wait.

When five minutes had passed and I had rung the bell once more, a face appeared before me. 'Yes?'

I stared at him. 'I've been standing here for over five minutes,' I said. 'While you've been sitting there chatting but well aware of my presence. My name is Catherine Cookson; I have an appointment with the bank manager. Will you inform him that I am now going to transfer my account? Good morning!'

Before I reached home, there was a car at the door with the manager pleading his cause, but I would have none of it. It didn't matter about me being Catherine Cookson; it didn't matter that I had a lot of money in the bank. I could have been Mrs Bloggs, Mrs Brown, Mrs Black, Mrs White, I said. They would have treated that person in the same way. Any person who put money into his bank deserved a little attention, if not courtesy. I was moving my account.

He begged me to reconsider, because my leaving under these circumstances would have repercussions on many people.

I was always influenced by the thought of unemployment. I reconsidered.

The only other time when I felt wild with the Westminster Bank was when a clerk attended to me while smoking a cigarette. I couldn't believe it. When I was sitting in the manager's office a few minutes later, I made no reference to it. But somebody must have, because on my next visit there was no cigarette dangling from this clerk's lips.

The next incident I had connected with Nan Smith was frightening. I hadn't heard from her for a long time. She phoned me to say she had just come back from Ireland and had a present for me for Christmas; would I come and get it? She was then living in one of the big houses on the front in St Leonards. I told her we were going home for Christmas to Tom's people, so I wouldn't have the time. Then she begged me to come because this present wouldn't keep.

Tom said, 'You'd better go. But what is she after? She hasn't bothered you since she's in the big money.'

Within a few minutes of having met her, I learned that her husband Sammy had walked out on her some months previously. I didn't know the reason then. We were still rationed: butter, sugar and everything else was very scarce. The present she had for me was a half pound of bacon, a half pound of butter and a piece of cheap dress material. I couldn't believe that she'd brought me all this way on a winter's night for this. When I was about to leave, she picked up a parcel and said she was going along to her friends' at the end of the road, who were estate agents, and she'd walk with me to the bus.

When we got outside, she walked slowly, chatting amicably, and waited for the bus. She waved me away, and I was puzzled because her manner was so bright and cheery.

I had noticed a car on the opposite side of the road near the promenade. I saw it again when the bus stopped in the centre of the town when I had to get off to take another bus for the rest of the journey home. What made me notice the car was that it didn't continue straight on behind the bus up Queens Road but turned and parked opposite where I was waiting for the Parker Road bus that would take me to the outskirts of the town.

When I got off the bus at Parker Road, there was the car again. It was dark and I had half a mile to go to reach the house. I took to my heels and ran. I battered on the front door then fell past Tom gasping, 'There are two men; they've been following me in a car from Nan's.'

'What have you got in the basket?' he said.

I showed him. 'It must be customs,' he said. 'She's up to something.'

Oh yes, I knew then that she had been up to something.

As I thrust the butter and bacon into the corner of the pantry with the material, the hall bell rang. Tom went and opened the door and there were a plain-clothes policeman and a customs officer, who asked if they could come in.

I was questioned. Yes, I had been along to Mrs Smith's, but all she had given me was some bacon and butter and a lot of material . . . Could they see it? I showed them and then I said, 'Look, search this house from top to bottom, you'll find nothing here. Oh yes, I forgot, there's a pair of fleecy-lined boots she sold me some time ago. I think she got them in Ireland, but go on, go on – the house is yours.'

I was in a state. It was strange, but it was from this incident that I really got to know Nan's character.

They searched the house then. Standing in the kitchen again in front of two very frightened people – because Tom, too, was shaking inwardly – they said, 'She's been bringing stuff over from Ireland by all ways and means: material, watches, food et cetera. She had her husband conning watches for a time, but he opted out.'

I could see she was still playing big Diamond Lil, plying her estate agent and doctor friends with things they couldn't get in England. She had made so many trips to Ireland that she came under suspicion. She had even appeared pregnant at one time. But why had she sent for me that night? I know now she wanted to involve me, strip me of my respectability and, of course, get Tom into trouble. It was many, many years later when I realised that this was one way of getting her own back. But what did she think I would get for receiving half a pound of butter and bacon and a small piece of cheap dress material?

We went to Tom's for Christmas, but we had a most miserable time because we didn't know what the outcome would be. The outcome was that she was fined. I heard nothing further.

Now I go back to the day of her visit, and it was odd that the very next afternoon, who should knock at the door but Mrs Webster. How I disliked that woman, but there she was. She wanted me to take her on again because if I didn't she'd have to go back to London, and there was only the Salvation Army for her. Well, the Salvation Army or whatever could take her – she was one load I wasn't going to carry on my back again.

Nan's bankruptcy case dragged on and on. I understood she was allowed to stay in the big house on the front until the business was finalised. During this time, I was picking up my first burden again. I learned that my mother was so ill, she wasn't expected to live very long. She had been cook-general at Dr Carstair's house for years – another doctor so caring that he came in the car every morning just after seven and took her to do the chores when she could hardly stand. Her ankles were as thick as her thighs. They were so fond of Kate. What they meant was they were fond of her work – and she could work. She kept everybody's house clean except her own. Anyway, the outcome of this was that I brought her home to Hastings to die. The doctor gave her a fortnight: I kept her alive for three years. She was a year in The Hurst, then we moved to Loreto[5] in 1954, and in 1956 she died. I was free at last. And I began my first autobiography – for I needed to get so much out of my system. Little did I think the task would take twelve years – and still my system wasn't cleared. You can't get rid of the subconscious.

---

5 Catherine and Tom's home in Hastings until they moved North in 1976.

9

Back to the doctors again. Healthwise, it seemed everything was wrong with me at this period, not only bleeding at both ends, but my tongue was really having a go too. You know the saying, 'Hold your tongue'? Well, it's very difficult to do that, practically speaking. Then there was the pain under my eyes. My cheekbones were so sore that I couldn't touch them at times.

What was it?

I was standing in front of that desk again.

'Catarrh. Use a spray,' he said. 'Everybody gets catarrh; it's the sea air.'

'I thought the sea air cleared the passages.'

'Well, something's stopping yours up then, isn't it?'

I put up with the pain for months. I tried inhalants, I tried everything, but to no avail.

Again, I was standing before the desk.

'What! Still stuffy up there?'

'Yes, I'm still stuffy up there and I'm in pain most of the time.'

'Oh, well, let's have a look.'

He had a look and what he said was, 'My God! You've got a bloody great antrum.'

Antrim, to my knowledge, was a county in Ireland.

'What's an antrim?'

He glanced sideways at me, remembering the mastitis business, then went to his desk and said, 'It's antrum – ducts that are blocked up.' Then softening a little, he said, 'Well, now, seeing as you've had this for some long time, I think you'd better have it seen to, eh? I'll make an appointment for you to go to the hospital.'

'What for?'

The softness disappeared. 'To have an op, of course.'

Some time later, I got a notice from the hospital to occupy a bed there in ten days' time.

Now I'm going to jump backward.

I had for some long time been reading every book I could on self-help, philosophy and anything that might give me a lead to relieving at least one of my ailments. I had become friendly with a woman who attended the writers' circle. She was a very nervy individual, but who was I to look down on anybody with nerves . . . ? She had, I knew, been attending the House of Healing for some time. This was a big house situated about the old town, and I understood it was run by mediums and spiritualists and odd people like that. I wanted no truck along those lines at that time.

However, desperate ailments require desperate remedies – and I found myself one for the antrum, lying on a couch very like a doctor's surgery bed, in a quiet room that looked very normal and Christian with a crucifix hanging on the wall. But what didn't appear normal to me was the little Welsh woman who buzzed around me. As I have said in my earlier writings, I'm not fond of little women because from my younger days in Harton Workhouse I suffered under one, and this little individual almost made me leap from that couch when, standing behind me and placing her hands on my head, she said, 'Stop being sorry for yourself. You're not the only one who was born on the wrong side of the blanket.'

Now, as far as I knew, no one except the matron in the Institution, Nan Smith and my writers' circle friend knew that I was illegitimate. Then she went on to tell me about myself while her fingers brought excruciating pain from my cheekbones.

I had understood that these kinds of people, when they laid their hands on you, caused you no pain. All I wanted at that moment was to get off that table and away, and I swore this would be the last time the House of Healing would see me.

What I remember next was standing at a bus stop with the tears rolling down my face. It was bitterly cold and I was shivering. When I got off the bus at Pine Avenue, I was still crying.

Now this is the strange thing. I cannot remember anything that happened after. This took place on a Friday night and what filled that weekend is a blank. But on the Monday morning, I recall being in the bathroom, bending over the washbowl and sluicing my face with water and all of a sudden I became rigid. I slowly turned and looked in the mirror. Was this me? For I hadn't been able to sluice my face like that for over a year. I rubbed my cheekbones and there was no sign of pain nor swelling. I realised I'd not given the antrum a thought since I had got off that bus and walked up Pine Avenue on Friday night.

I have never felt it since, and that was forty-four years ago.

What I did recall that morning was the reason why I went to the House of Healing in the first place. We had a greengrocer who used to deliver the fruit and vegetables, and after a different man had done the delivery for a fortnight, I said to him, 'Have you been on your holidays?' Shaking his head, he replied, 'No, Mrs Cookson, not on a holiday. I've been in hospital and if I had known then what I know now, that place wouldn't have seen me. I've been through some pain in my life, but never anything like what I've experienced lately.'

'You've had an operation?' I said.

'Yes,' he replied. 'It sounds so simple. I've had what you call an antrum at the top of my nose and it was giving me gip, so the doctor thought I'd better have it cleared out. But I didn't know what I was in for.'

When I told him I was going in for the same thing, he said, 'Don't you do it, Mrs Cookson. Don't you do it.' And that's what really got me to visit the House of Healing.

Another strange thing happened there. Although the little bossy woman had cured my antrum – and she definitely had – I was still fearful of what she and the other healers represented. So when I was asked to join a sitting, I did so quite blindly – not knowing what a sitting really was.

At the time, I was in the process of writing my second book and suffering hard criticism from Tom.

'You can't use words like that; people won't understand them,' he'd say. 'If you want your book read widely, you've got to drop these North Country phrases. And look' – his finger would point – 'the predicate is wrong parse for that sentence.' Or it might be, 'You can't make a statement like that; that clause is out of place.' Or, 'Look, take the root word.' One time, when it got to the gerund and the gerundive, in order to stem my hurt feelings and the tears falling, I tried to be funny by saying, 'So it is, or is it – ain't?' but the schoolmaster was not moved.

One way and another, my entry into the literary world caused me a lot of tears and many was the time I cried bitterly over Tom's criticism, for it was harsh. He seemed to forget that he had been very fortunate in being a scholar at Oxford. He had every possible chance of studying grammar. For my part, if it sounded right, it was good enough for me.

But I knew something would have to be done. There had to be a compromise. So, 'All right,' I said. 'You set me a lesson in grammar each day and see where we'll get to.'

He did this, and now I'm grateful for it because I learned to parse a sentence. I learned where to place adjectives; I learned about verbs. I learned a little about clauses and a very little about the gerunds and gerundives. And what I learned I transferred to my writing . . .

I became very unhappy about it because suddenly my characters were speaking grammatically. My prose was correct and stilted. I was losing something and I knew it, but I wanted to please him. I also very much wanted to learn. But as time went on, I lost my verve.

Then came the night I was sitting in a ring in the House of Healing and two strange things happened. Opposite me was the medium; she went into a sort of quiet trance and began to give messages, but hesitantly. Then she said, 'There is someone trying to get a message through here, but it isn't to you.' This was to the person she had been speaking to.

She tried again to give another message, and again she stopped and said, 'Has anyone here lost someone by their own hand of late?' No one spoke. I remember wishing I was out of this; it was weird, eerie. My mind began to criticise; they were a lot of cranks. I was in a bad enough state of nerves without being among this crew. Such were my thoughts when her voice hit me, saying, 'There's someone . . . It's a man; he's standing behind . . .' And she pointed. I looked from side to side and the medium spoke to the woman next to me, saying, 'Have you lost anyone who has passed over by their own hand?' And the reply was, 'No.' Then she came to me and before she had finished I said, 'No, no.'

She seemed confused, then once again she started to give out messages, but her voice was loud now. She said, 'This person wants to get a message through, and it is to someone over there.' And now her finger was pointing straight at me. 'He wants to tell you . . .' She paused before ending, 'That you mustn't worry anymore about him, that it was done in a moment of weakness and he thanks you for thinking about him.' As she spoke enlightenment flashed. 'John Cole.'

I had known this man since I first came to Hastings. He was very ambitious and I think he would have married me if I had been a trained nurse – that's if I would have had him – because he started a house for rich old gentlemen who brought their antique furniture with them. He later married a state-registered nurse who was running the house for him, and I was at their reception after their quiet wedding. But money went to his head and, I understood, he took to gambling and got mixed up with an army type and got dreadfully into debt. Then one day, he went down into the coach house and blew his brains out. I was terribly upset about this; it had happened more than a year ago, yet at times I would think about him. So now I burst out, 'Yes, yes. I understand.'

The medium sighed and the business of messages went on, and then I was startled by her finger once again pointing at me. 'There's a very old man; he could be Indian,' she said.

Oh my God! Why had messages always had to come through Indians?

'He says,' she went on, 'that you must go your own way. You must put things down and go back to where you were; only then will you achieve anything . . . Do you understand?'

Did I understand? I was utterly amazed and I was no longer afraid. I accepted the message as if the person was standing in front of me – it seemed so natural.

I couldn't get out of that place quickly enough to get to Tom.

He happened to be at scouts and I went straight to the grammar school to meet him, and when I blurted out the message, strangely he didn't turn a hair. What he said was that he had known for some time that if I was to write, it had to be in my own way.

But nevertheless, I wanted his help – I needed his help. So from then on, when I finished a book, he would read it and give advice to the effect, 'I think that would be better put in this way or that.'

I have been published for thirty-four years now, and he's the only one who has ever given me any help at all. In fact, looking back right to my beginning, I had no help from anyone; no one to turn to ask for advice – literary or otherwise. So I was pleased to let him become my mentor. But for me, my writing had to be along the lines of my own thoughts, gained through my own experiences.

I said I cried a great deal through criticism, and not only from Tom. One day, I was writing in the study, which had a window looking out onto the drive, and to my surprise I saw coming down it a Mrs Oxenford. She had been a member of the writers' circle during the time I was secretary.

I invited her in warmly, yet wondering why she should pay me a visit. I can't remember now what the object of her visit was; I think it was to ask me to join something or other, but I do remember her looking down on my desk and saying, 'You do write them yourself then?'

'What do you mean, I do write them myself?'

I can see her thin smile as she replied, 'Well, they all say in the circle that Tom writes your stories for you.'

'*What!*'

'Well, that's what has been said.'

There it was again. No intellectual credit could be given to anyone who had worked in a laundry for almost fifteen years, and who sometimes made slips in grammar, such as pronouncing the 'w' in 'wholly', and who had not been able to translate a French phrase while reading a short story submitted by one of the circle who was afraid to read it herself.

I was so upset about this, but then it was just part of the pattern. I was an oddity because, as I said, whoever heard of a laundry worker – that's how I was termed – being able to write?

It may appear odd, but it was on very rare occasions that I had wet my hands in those long laundry years; I did it only when I was defiantly showing someone that I wouldn't ask them to do something that I couldn't do myself.

But now my doctor had something to hang onto. I was a writer. So everything that happened to me was put down to my temperament, plus the breakdown, which, of course, was again the result of my temperament. And all his theories about me were confirmed when I told him I wasn't going to have the operation for the antrum. He forgot that he had put a name to my pain and discomfort because now it had cleared up it was all due to my imagination.

I decided to leave him. I didn't know I was making a mistake by jumping out of the frying pan and into a very hot fire. To this day, I have a feeling of antipathy to women doctors, and who could blame me after twenty years of neglect?

But before I made the change, there was the business of the hysterectomy. I had twice been into hospital for a scrape and, when it did nothing to prevent the flow of blood, I was once again sent to the specialist. He took one look at me and said, impatiently as I recall, 'Oh, you'll just have to have the whole lot out.' This was towards 1955. My mother was with me, pottering about the house, happier than she had been in her life before, yet I was still fearful that she would take it into her head to go out one day and I knew what the result would be. Under doctor's orders, she had to be in bed from noon each day, but the job was to get her there.

At this time, I was hitting rock bottom, yet when J. Arthur Rank[6] said they wanted to turn my latest effort, *A Grand Man*, into a film and would I go to Ireland and set the scene and do the first script, how could I refuse?

I was feeling very ill when I returned home, so a date was set for my entry into hospital to have the hysterectomy.

But it was at this juncture I was to be given further evidence of the power of spiritual healing. As I have said before, it has never created any miracles for me, but it has led me to help myself. It's a case of, I think, as Christ said, 'The Kingdom of God is within you.' So to me, all power is there.

One day, a Sunday, I was lying on the couch in the drawing room. Tom was outside mowing the lawn, and I was feeling desperately ill. I was due to go into hospital in six days' time. I was very worried about the hysterectomy because I imagined in those days it would mean the end of our sex life. I was weighed down with guilt at the thought that

---

6   Founder of British film company the Rank Organisation, and one of the most important figures in the British film industry at this time.

having deprived Tom of children, I would now no longer be able to be a wife to him.

I digress again, but with regard to having another shot at pregnancy, when I was about forty-two and in the Buchanan Hospital in the centre bed of the ward, I was approached by this big, burly individual. I asked him in a very quiet voice if it would be possible that I could carry a baby if I stayed for the nine months in bed. He walked away up the ward yelling – and he did yell – 'Don't be silly woman, you're past it. Even if you weren't, you know there's no chance.'

I burned with anger as I cried with humiliation.

When this man, at a later date, examined me, I was put in mind of a passage in a book I'd read where the author describes an innocent girl being dragged from the streets and stamped as a prostitute after being examined by a so-called doctor who stuck an iron instrument into her fore-body. I think it was the French police at that time who got so much a head for bringing in a prostitute, and any woman walking alone on the streets was fair game. That particular examination – and that particular doctor – brought that scene vividly to mind. By, I've known some doctors, haven't I?

This took place again in the Buchanan Hospital in Hastings. Yet I'm grateful to this hospital for, some years later, this was where I experienced a pre-med for the first time in my life, eliminating my fear of being wheeled down into the slaughterhouse. That is no exaggeration of my acquaintance with hospital theatres.

But here I was on this lovely Sunday afternoon, lying watching Tom through the window, when all of a sudden I felt the most urgent need to get up, go into the garden and put my hands into the soil.

A few minutes later, when Tom saw me kneeling on the concrete path in my nightie pulling weeds out of the flower border, he thought I had gone mad. When he tried to lift me up, I said quietly, 'Leave me alone, Tom. I'm all right. Now just leave me alone.'

I worked on that border for an hour, and my mother thought I had flipped again too.

The following day, I did the same thing, only for longer. The third day, I worked all morning, not kneeling now, but bending down. That afternoon, I wrote a letter to the hospital saying I wouldn't be having the operation.

I have still got my ovaries and I've had no trouble with them since.

The result of spiritual healing, or the power of thought . . . I have eight ailments at the present time, and it has helped me to cope with most of them; even now, it is helping me to come to terms with losing most of the sight in my left eye.

But back to my new doctor. She was young, had just got her degree and was the wife of a friend of Tom's – at least, I should say of an associate of Tom's. Tom made very few friends. A lot of men would speak to him as a friend, but in all honesty, as he says now, there were few he liked. Anyway, what should I do but transfer myself onto her book?

How is it that converts are more Catholic than those bred in the bone? Of course, I didn't know that she was a Catholic then, nor that she knew that I had left the Church. But I found out when she invited Tom and me to tea and there was a priest waiting for me.

It was a very stormy tea table. I pointed out strongly to that priest that I was no lapsed Catholic – lapsed Catholics were lazy individuals who hoped to be lucky enough to have the last rites. Or there were those who went to their Easter duties once a year and that was that. No, I said, I was no longer a Catholic and had no intention of returning to the faith. It was from that moment that the doctor–patient relationship became very strained. She, of course, had all my medical history from the previous man, and hadn't I had a breakdown?

She had been so piously sweet to me when I visited that surgery, but now all was changed. The bleeding from my nose and my tongue she put down to offshoots of the menopause. She didn't believe that it had been going on from when I was eighteen. But inadvertently, she was the means to finding out exactly why I had been bleeding all this time.

One morning – some years later – looking in the mirror, I saw below my hairline a large purple-red blotch about a quarter of an inch long, a smaller one on my cheek, and one on my lower lip. They were the same marks I had all down the side of my tongue, only larger. When I showed them to her, her response was, 'Oh, I've got a spot on my nose. There's a skin specialist coming to the Frederick Road Infirmary; I must go and see about it. I'll give you a note to see him too.'

I have described a meeting with this man in my autobiography – how he called in another doctor and nurses and asked had anyone seen marks like this on a patient before. No one had. He described them as the outward signs of an inherited vascular disease known as telangiectasia.

I was asked if I would go before a panel of doctors. I did so gladly. There were about twenty of them, and no one knew anything about the disease except the doctor in question. He was very kind. He must have remembered that when he asked me if there were any bleeders on my mother's side, I had said no. But when he asked if there were any on my father's side, I had, for the first time, defiantly applied the word illegitimate to myself. The result of this investigation by the doctors was that one asked me how it was to feel unique. My answer was it was 'Pretty bloody'.

The bouts of bleeding could be very heavy at times. When it eventually clotted, I would sit, afraid to move for hours. There have been nights when I've sat in the study, Tom with me for twelve hours at a stretch, only moving to go to the lavatory, and very slowly at that. But when the blood wouldn't clot, Tom would take me to hospital. There was one day when he was called from school, and when he got me to the outpatients' department, I had to wait my turn. Then a young doctor questioned me. Was I allergic to drugs? I was. Had I ever had my nose cauterised?

Oh yes, I had.

I didn't describe the day I had it done in St Albans without a local anaesthetic, and later stood against the wall howling my eyes out. A woman passing thought I had lost someone in the war. When I told her I'd had a bleeding stopped in my nose, she exclaimed, 'Oh, that,' and went on her way.

The young doctor said he would try to find somebody who would see to me, and I was put in a side ward. It was now three o'clock on a Friday afternoon. There was another bed in the ward and into it came an old gypsy woman surrounded by her entire family. When they were asked to leave, she turned on her side and talked at me. She talked and talked and I, my nose and throat being clotted with blood, couldn't answer her. I did a dumb show, pointing to my mouth and nose.

When her family returned later, Tom was sitting by my side, and one by one they came and commiserated with him because his poor wife could not talk.

'Has someone hit her?'

'No.'

'Has she hit a bus?'

'No.'

'Why all the blood about her face, then?'

'She has a kind of disease.'

'Oh, a disease . . . *a disease*.'

There followed a conference round the gypsy's bed. Tom and I exchanged glances; we wanted to laugh, but I was in no state for laughter.

I don't know what the matter was with the old girl, but she went out the next morning in the middle of all her family. Before she left she gave me a present – two bananas. By that afternoon, I was longing for her return, for a little woman of uncertain age was brought into the ward who was thoroughly enjoying her illness and must have been for a long time. She was well known in the hospital; I think she had had some form of cancer.

The curtains were drawn around her, and the young doctor came in and, if I've ever heard anyone being seduced, it was then. Apparently, from the conversation, he had dealt with her before. And later, she didn't talk to me but to the ceiling about her conquests.

It was now Saturday night and I hadn't seen a doctor, but I'd been told they were mostly off for the weekend and they had tried to contact somebody in Brighton or Eastbourne who knew about blood, but without any success.

On Sunday, I couldn't stand the sex kitten any longer. I got up and went into the sister's office where the young doctor happened to be and said I was going home. When the doctor asked why, I smilingly said I couldn't stand listening to him being near-raped again. At this, he said, 'She can't help it. She's a very sick woman.' And I answered, 'Yes, in more ways than one.'

Before I left, he promised that he would try to get in touch with a doctor who knew something about my trouble.

He was as good as his word.

The following Wednesday, a doctor called at the house – he was from Brighton. He was an elderly man and very nice. He said he had heard vaguely about this disease, but nothing could be done for it. 'And, my dear' – he patted my hand, reminding me very much of the doctor who got the stuff all the way from France before the fall – 'My dear, you'll have to consider yourself an invalid for the rest of your life. When you have these bleedings, you must go to bed and remain very quiet until you recover your strength in order to get gently about.'

So that was that. I was to be an invalid for the rest of my life. No more gardening, no more clearing woodland, no more sawing . . . That was my only recreation: an hour's sawing a day to keep the fire going. I used to get great satisfaction out of this. I think it stemmed back from those early days gathering wood from the slacks and being a natural beachcomber. And, of course, my platform career was finished.

Strangely, I was in demand these days to talk. But, poor soul that I was, I always had to sit while addressing an audience because I had rheumatics in my legs – I put this out to save my face because my nerves were in such a state that I couldn't stand and face an audience – and this was five years after the breakdown, when I had lost the use of my legs for a time.

But if I was to die from bleeding, then I told myself it wouldn't happen by lying in bed. I was going to carry on as normally as possible, and I did.

10

In those early days, I was getting more and more requests to give talks here and there across the country. I think I could write a book alone on the people I talked to and my reception by them.

There was the very, very hot day I travelled into the heart of Sussex, as usual not feeling very well. I'd been asked to speak to a women's group affiliated to a church. I walked about a mile and a half from the bus stop and arrived at what appeared to be a little deserted village. But not quite deserted, for there in the schoolroom sat two old women – really old women – surrounded by a squad of children.

'Where would I find the minister's wife?' I asked.

'Oh, she be in the fields.'

'In the fields?'

'Yes, with the rest of 'em.'

'Gonna be a storm, see. Couldn't let the hay lie there 'n get wet, could you, now?' Was I the wife who had come to give 'em a talk?

Yes, I was the wife who had come to give them a talk.

Well, I'd better get on with it then, hadn't I?

So I got on with it, but not in my usual style. I just sat chatting to them about my early life et cetera, and at the end I remember one of them, grinning broadly, said, 'You be like us after all, no better no worse, eh?'

Yes, I was like them, no better no worse. They made me a cup of tea. I travelled a mile and a half down to the bus. I never met the parson's wife or my audience, or had a thank-you letter.

At the other end of the scale, some years later I addressed almost 2000 people in a hall mainly filled with women from the WI. Why, I ask at this juncture – and I am speaking to the heads of this society – do you not hold a short course to train chairwomen, or chairpersons, or whatever you might call them? How often have I sat on a platform, or below it, waiting to start my talk and listening to a woman yammering on, calling up the knitting circle, sewing circle, the one who was organising a trip to the theatre, or asking who would take charge of stalls at the coming garden fete, or wanting volunteers to organise this, that or the other. My talks would generally be set to begin at three o'clock, and the time allowed was three quarters of an hour to an hour. I always arrived early as I had to travel by train or bus, and many of the places were isolated, with an infrequent service. There I would be, sitting from the beginning of the proceedings, sometimes sweating in the summer and shivering in the winter. And only on rare occasions did I begin at the appointed time.

At one particular WI, it was a very, very hot summer day: the windows were all open, and there was the hum of a threshing machine coming from the fields. In the front row sat three perspiring women, fanning their open-necked blouses with papers. They were all, as I remember, very big busted. They looked hot and tired. They had scrambled in at the last moment, likely after having got their husbands' dinner. Anyway, there they sat, grinning at me until I began to talk, then one after another they nodded off. Well, you see, this was my third appearance at this WI in the past five years and they were likely telling themselves they had heard it all before. But no, it was a different talk I was giving, but the voice was just the same, and gradually they fell into a relaxing sleep. Of course, I was the only one who could see them, as I had the platform to myself. Then one of them gave a loud snorting snore and the whole room burst into laughter, in which I joined. At that, the three of them woke up and clapped vigorously, which sent some of the audience into hysterics and me collapsing onto the chairwoman's chair – I was able to stand at this juncture of my platform career – then the roof almost shot off when one of them turned round and asked the woman behind her, quite loudly, 'Well, did she say something funny?'

I liked that group very much. They asked me again the following year, but I thought enough was as good as a feast. But they continued to ask me down the years, and my excuse was not an excuse anymore, as I had become too ill to travel.

Then there were the Business and Professional Women's dinners. The first one I attended was on the coast. It was a long journey and I was being put up for the night at a member's house. I arrived there, changed, and was taken to a hall and into a cocktail do. Then came the procession into the main dining hall. Talk about the Mayor and Corporation – definitely the Mayor and Corporation were present, not counting the leading lights of a number of other Business and Professional Women's clubs.

We dignitaries were all arrayed at a very long table; I was sitting next to the president, or whatever she called herself. What followed was a dinner; what followed that was the introduction by the president of the other presidents sitting along the table, and one after the other they got up and said their piece. I understood it was to be well planned, with a few speeches only. I think there were eight – and none stuck to the time limit.

We had started dinner at seven o'clock. At half past nine, I was still sitting there waiting my turn. I was never able to eat anything before giving a talk. As for drinking, no alcoholic beverages were allowed to pass my lips in those days – the memory of Kate was still too strong on me. After the last lady had sat down, there was an interval, so it was ten o'clock before I started to speak to a now very warmed-up – wine- and spirit-wise – audience.

As a result of this evening, I got a number of requests to be guest speaker at annual events. One I recall with anything but amusement finally put me off Business and Professional Women's dos. I was in the West Country, and again I went through all the ceremony. Again, the chairwomen of the various clubs had no idea of the time. Again, there was an interval, but when following this the president didn't stand up to announce me, I realised there was something else forthcoming. I said to her, 'When do I give this talk?'

Smilingly, she pointed to the menu, 'Haven't you seen the back of it, my dear?'

No, I hadn't looked at the back of the menu.

'You're on at the end. You see, last year we had a cabaret, but we were advised to have you to jolly things up a bit and send us all away laughing.'

It was near eleven o'clock when I got to my feet. I could have talked about Madam Chiang Kai-shek, Stalin, Charlie Chaplin or Houdini, it wouldn't have made much difference. The majority of them were tight, some politely so, some not politely so. I cut what I had to say very short. I didn't send them away laughing. I had been at that table from seven o'clock in the evening; it was twelve when we left the hall. We were accompanied by a so-called distinguished member of the town, who was a friend of the people with whom I was staying. He insisted on talking. He wanted to know how I wrote, why I wrote, how easy it was to write. Out of courtesy for my hosts, I had to be civil to him, for he seemed of importance to them. I got to bed somewhere around two o'clock; I had left home at noon the day before. That was the last Business and Professional Women's conference I ever spoke to.

In nearly thirty years of giving talks long and short and doing after-dinner speeches, I think there weren't more than half a dozen that left me feeling like that one did.

I've had some great days on the platform. Two of the highest were my talks to The Swanwick Writers' Summer School and Ashington

Festival. When it was known I was to speak at the festival, different societies in the surrounding towns came on bus trips. And so, from an ordinary hall that they had booked, they had to take another and yet another to accommodate those who wanted to be there on the night.

Two days prior to the festival, I had to give a talk in Nelson [in Lancashire] and this was very successful – I always classed the talks as successful when the audience both laughed and cried. On our journey from Nelson to Ashington, Tom decided to take a detour to a place called Alston [a town in Cumbria, approximately 1000 miles above sea level]. This nearly saw the finish of me, as it was in Aston that I discovered I really had a phobia: acrophobia – the fear of heights and great open spaces. I understood then why I'd always wanted a walled garden. It all tends, I think, to the lack of security I felt in my early years. I was crouched on the bottom of the car crying my eyes out while Tom was saying, 'Try to sit up and look at this; it's wonderful. You'll never see anything like this again.' I never wanted to see anything like that again. My heart was beating so fast, I thought I would die.

As the journey went on, the feeling became worse, for the land became higher and fell away on either side into infinity. Eventually, he said, 'We are on a flat piece. You'll be all right here.' He hauled me out of the car and I sat on the running board, and there opposite me, across a piece of broken ground, was a derelict house that had once been an inn for the drovers. It was miles from anywhere, and as I stared at it through swollen eyelids, the story of *The Mallen Streak* was born, for it was in that house, sheltering from a storm, that the lovers come together and the real tragedy of the Mallens begins.

Eventually, when we got down to level ground we stopped at a kiosk and Tom phoned my cousin in Birtley, where we were going to stay. The telephone box was situated at a fork in a road surrounded by woodlands. Little did I know that twelve years later, I'd be living not a stone's throw from that kiosk. For all I wanted at that moment was to get away and into the civilisation of a town. And all the while Tom was driving, I kept saying, 'I'll never be able to make it tomorrow night. I'll have to tell them at Ashington; I feel so ill.'

But I made it, and it was another splendid evening. After the talk, I signed books for two hours; in fact, the bus drivers complained that they could wait no longer, and if their passengers didn't come, they were leaving.

Then there was the talk I gave in a theatre in Sussex. The hall was packed except for the front row: only two people sat there, an old lady and gentleman, both county types. He kept his hands on top of his walking stick placed between his knees; she sat stiffly erect. My talk that night was to be divided into two parts; it was called, 'Me Granda versus Lord Chesterfield'. The first part of this talk was reminiscing about my early days, the trials and the tears, and the laughter, but mostly dealing with the character of old John. Well, while the rest of the audience laughed loudly or were subdued into deep sympathy, there was no emotion shown by the couple in the front row. His eyes were fixed upon me; he looked for all the world like a bristling colonel, and his white moustache was the only thing that seemed to move.

There followed a short interval, during which I thought, 'Well, when I get onto Lord Chesterfield and his class, that might bring some movement from the old couple.' For they were, him especially, a bit unnerving. I had taught myself the art of public speaking: do your homework and you won't need to refer to notes.

I began the second half by saying, 'I will now come to the life of Lord Chesterfield as I see it.' I got no further, for the colonel had moved; his stick rapped twice on the floor and he glared up at me crying, 'Never mind Lord Chesterfield, give us more of your granda.' This caused a roar, and so poor Lord Chesterfield didn't have an airing that night. I gave him more of my granda. But it just goes to show, as I told myself then, and had done many times before, never to judge people on their appearance or think you know what they'd like to hear.

Tom always made it his business to be at the station to meet me, no matter what time of night it was after I had been away talking. It was snowing heavily on the night I went to talk to the Rotary Club along the coast. My invitation had been so courteous: they were going to invite another lady so I wouldn't feel lost among all the men. What a pity the courtesy didn't hold up.

There were about forty or more men present, and the majority sat at both sides of a long table. I was in the middle at one side, and at the end to my left two men sat counting money and discussing accounts – it was a very odd arrangement. I couldn't believe it when they still continued as I started to speak. And when the rattling of their money and their undercover talk began to have an effect on me, I stopped and looked towards them. One of the men present at the table, addressing them, said, 'Let up a bit.' They did let up, but not entirely.

I swore that was the last time I would address a solely male audience. And they were the first words I said to Tom when he met me in the station hall. We hadn't a car at the time: we had to take the bus and trudge the rest of the way home in the snow. It was midnight when we got in. My fee was two pounds.

But then there was the day I faced another completely male audience in the Pier Restaurant in St Leonards. There were about fifty of them, all parsons or ministers as they are called in the Methodist Church, and I've never had a happier time or a more appreciative gathering.

And what does it feel like when 600 women get to their feet to give you a standing ovation? This happened in the Civic Centre in Newcastle. The restaurant is only supposed to hold 500, but they had managed to squeeze in another hundred, and I was told another hundred were disappointed.

Women can be bitches. I've had so much personal experience of this. But women can also be friendly and warm creatures. I had learned to gauge an audience, and I judged that day that some of the ladies in the Ladies' Circle Conference weren't actually in favour of me. Well, after all, what was I? A girl who had worked in a laundry, illegitimate, with that awful upbringing, and there I was, standing and addressing them as if born to it. I mean, well. Oh, she has made her name as a novelist, yes, but nevertheless . . . When I told them how I had come to make my name as a novelist, when I didn't hide any of my low upbringing, when I brought out that the fears and desires in me were in them too, I saw them melt: one of them cried, and there they stood with the rest.

It was strange too, that on that day as I stood on the dais, there should be a plaque behind me on which were inscribed the names of all the mayors that had graced the council chamber of Newcastle, and on almost head level with me was the name 'Cookson'. Of course, it's only my name through marriage, but nevertheless I felt pride in it.

There was also the time when a friend of mine asked me would I go and speak to the Over Sixties Club in the Methodist church in Hastings? I had always been partial to Methodists because of the way they put things over. Priests I considered didactic, parsons yammered, but Methodists talked. I was to start my talk at three o'clock, and the hall was full. The chairwoman was on her feet, and she was to beat all the WI chairwomen into a frazzle. She gave detailed points of the last outing, then she greeted different members who had been ill and heard their personal replies. But her big moment was in welcoming visitors from abroad. Someone from Australia or Timbuktu or suchlike places, and these people in turn stood up and said their pieces. By this time, the audience was looking towards me – I was sitting on a form to the side of the platform – and I said to my friend, 'I thought I was to speak at three o'clock.' She said, 'Oh, that woman.' And went to see if she could do anything about it. Someone approached the lady on the platform; she stopped, glanced towards me, then went on with what she considered her business. At something to four, she announced that they would be stopping shortly to have tea. Quietly, I enquired when I was supposed to speak. My friend brought a member of the committee to me. Bending over me, she smiled and said, 'Well, the tea will only take ten minutes. How long do you intend to talk?' I said, 'Well, my talk usually takes anything up to an hour.' Oh, she was aghast. 'The hall has to be cleared by half past four,' she said, 'for the others coming in. Anyway, it'll give you time to say a few words to them, eh?' I rose to my feet, smiled at her and said, 'Another time, perhaps,' and walked out. It was the only time I ever did that, and I felt justified.

So much for my talking career.

11

Nan Smith had been out of my life for some time, until one day, as Tom and I were looking round the ground floor in Dunk's saleroom, I felt someone staring at me from a dim corner – it looked like an old woman sitting there among boxes and old junk. Then Tom's voice came low, saying, 'That's Nan.'

I couldn't believe it. I had always been dress-conscious, and was constantly trying to get her to dress decently, but she had never kept herself very smart – until she came into property and then she went mad for a time. During one of our very lean times after the war, I met her in the town and she was wearing an Aquascutum coat – or so she told me – and high, fur-lined boots, and she had looked extremely smart; wealthily smart. They had likely been bought in Ireland. But now there was this huddled bundle of drabness sitting in the corner. I remember saying, 'My God!' I could have added, 'How the mighty have fallen,' or 'Justice will out.'

Tom said, 'You must speak to her.' As I approached, she got to her feet, and a shadow of the old charm flashed through and she said, 'Hello there.'

'Hello, Nan, how are you?'

'Oh, you know, not too bad. I was having a look round. You get tired.'

She had always attended sales, but mostly in the basement where years ago she would buy a box or a basket of odds and ends for a couple of shillings, and she was always lucky to find quite good pieces of china or glass in them. But when she came into money, she frequented the first floor or upstairs in the antique rooms, and she filled her houses with furniture of all kinds.

She asked after my mother, and I told her she wasn't too well but I had a job to keep her in bed. She congratulated me on my latest book, and I thanked her. While filled with pity for her, I was also fearful that my pity would overturn my past experience and it would bring her back into my life.

It was rare that Tom and I could get out together during those three years Mother was with us because of my real fear that she would in some way manage to reach a bar or get someone to bring her spirits in. The only time I would leave the house would be if Tom was there to take over. So the routine was that I went out once a week to get her pension and her books from the library. This was one of the occasions when Tom met me from school and we both treasured the time. Then we had to come across Nan.

The thought of Nan's condition coloured the day for Tom and, ever forgiving, he said, 'Would you like to ask her up?'

'No. Never. Never. What on earth are you thinking of?'

It was some weeks later when I met her again – on the street this time. She looked no better, and asked plaintively if I would mind if she came up and saw Kate. What could I say?

She arrived some days later with a great big parcel of something. This was for Mam.

Mam greeted her warmly. I took tea in to them in the bedroom; she was ecstatic about the new house.

When we opened the parcel later, Mam couldn't believe her eyes at the sight of a lot of old, smelly clothes. But that was Nan. In a way, she was like a dog bringing you slippers or a bone. She couldn't go anywhere unless she took a gift – hadn't she filched money from me for years to supply her many friends with presents? One way of doing it was when

I gave her a cheque for a straight amount of pounds for the housekeeping, or for anything else, she would add on ten shillings. I didn't find this out until my little bank balance almost disappeared and my bank book and returns didn't tally.

I heaved a sigh of relief when she left the house. Although her present condition elicited pity, I couldn't unbend in her presence. I didn't want her to touch on my life again in any way. As she stood at the door, she looked about her, then turned to me and said quietly, 'You always said you cannot buy friendship; you've been proved right, as usual.' And at that she walked away up the drive looking like an old woman, bent and beaten.

For days afterwards, the atmosphere in the house seemed changed. Mother said, 'God help her! Whatever she's done, God help her!' And I thought, 'You cooperated with her. In a way, you were as bad as her. If you had only opened your eyes and seen Tom then as you do now, I would have been saved at least three years of hell.'

I've explained elsewhere how we just had to have a break, and we went to the Broads for a week only to come back to find that she had brought her end nearer by ordering whisky on the sly. On the day we came back, she held me close and begged me never to leave her again. The following Saturday night, I was sitting by her side watching her dying. She died on the Sunday morning.

Such were my mixed feelings about her and all that she had put me through from when she came onto my horizon when I was five years old, I shouldn't have had any guilty feelings concerning her. Yet I felt I should have talked more with her, shown her that I loved her by being demonstrative towards her, but I couldn't. What I also regretted was that I should have asked her point blank more about the man who was my father. Yet, all the while, part of me was thanking God that I was free at last.

There was about £80 insurance money. The funeral bill came to almost £50 – it would be £500 today. What was I to do with the rest?

Definitely not use a penny of it for myself. Strangely, I didn't want anything from her. She had many faults, but she had many qualities, and one of them was kindness and sharing. And so I knew that she would be pleased if I gave the rest of the money to old age pensioners. I didn't know anyone in my quarter of the town in need – although I'd no doubt many were. I didn't want to appear as a lady bountiful, so I went into St Leonards where, in a block of basement flats, lived, I understood, some men and women who had seen better days and were now on their own. I knocked at different doors, handed them a couple of pounds and walked away. They must have thought I was barmy. I remember saying such words as, 'That's a present from a friend.'

Came the day there was five pounds left.

Now what followed is absolutely true. I was sitting alone in the drawing room, my knees towards the fire – I was always cold. I was thinking about a new story when all of a sudden Kate's voice came to me from behind my chair. I knew she was there and I stiffened. And when she said, 'Forgive and forget, lass. Send Nan the five pounds. She's up against it, very much so.' I yelled aloud, 'No! No! She's not getting anything more out of me. And I want nothing more to do with her. No!'

I spun round. There was no one there. The next day, I put the five single pound notes into an envelope and wrote on a piece of paper without any heading, 'Don't thank me. Don't phone. And just remember I haven't gone soft again.'

I daren't tell Tom what I had done because, although he too pitied her – more than I did – he was also fearful of her presence and her effect on me.

Four days later, the phone rang and a tearful voice said, 'I can't help it. I've got to thank you. You don't know what you've done.' I answered coolly, curtly, 'Very well, but please, Nan, don't phone again. You know it's finished.'

'Yes, yes, I understand,' she said humbly.

I didn't know till later that when my letter arrived she had burned the last chair in the dreadful basement where she was living and kept her last shilling for the gas. She didn't usually open any mail because they were mostly brown envelopes. After she had seen what was in my letter, she lay on the floor and cried. I might have doubted this story had I not later seen the conditions under which she was living.

I cannot recall what message of hers or what circumstances got us to that basement. It was like a dungeon, with only a bed, a cupboard and a table in it. Apparently, she wouldn't have had these had one of the bailiff's men not taken pity on her when they cleared the house under the bank's orders, and left her these few sticks of furniture she had at one time thrown away into the basement. She was ill and had a dreadful cough, and I couldn't have seen a dog remain in those conditions.

Where had all her fine friends gone? I didn't ask, but we helped her to get a flat, and she pulled herself together and got a job looking after a little boy whose mother had a shop in the centre of the town. She seemed settled because, her usual charm revived, she made friends with her employer.

I saw very little of her for quite some time after this, but strangely, when we did meet, I could sense the bitterness in her. Perhaps it was because I was keeping her at arm's length while, as she said, making a name for myself. But of course, she had added, she knew I would; she had always known I was a writer.

Things did not go right with her new friend. Her dominating nature did not go down well with the woman, nor her slackness in looking after the house and the child, nor her continued smoking – she never drank – so she was once again on her own.

From the time we had found her in the basement, Tom had said to me, 'Do you want her back?' I recall going for him. Was he mad? He had said, 'But you are so sorry for her – she's a pathetic individual.' 'She may be,' I said, 'but she's still Nan, and I know the depths of her.'

But from then, I let her come up every Wednesday to tea; I filled a basket with groceries and Tom filled a sack with coal, then he drove her back to the flat. Gradually over this period, she said, 'I must do something for you. I can't take everything for nothing. Let me wash up.'

No, I wouldn't let her do anything like that, until one day she arrived when I wasn't well and that was the opportunity to go into the kitchen. From then on, she would insist on washing up.

It was some time later I met the young woman who had employed her and she gave me her side of what had happened. Nan was so domineering. She wanted to take over her life. She objected to her going out with her gentleman friend at night – she had been a widow for some time.

This woman undoubtedly wasn't like Miss McMullen. She put Mrs Nan Smith in her place and had told her to go . . .

I had working for me at that time a Mrs Stanbridge. She had been with me about seven years. As Nan's weekly visit became longer, she met up with Mrs Stanbridge and I know she spun her the tale of how we'd had a marvellous house together et cetera, et cetera. So I made it my business to put Mrs Stanbridge into the real picture.

We had a boat on the Cam in Cambridge, which should have been a source of relaxation, but the longest we ever spent on it was a fortnight. We had it for ten years and got to know a lot of the rivers. But I never spent a minute on it when I wasn't terrified, because I hate rivers. When we went on our boat trips, we would leave the house in charge of Mrs Stanbridge and Nan. As time went on, I noticed more and more that when we returned, hardly anything had been done in the house and there were vases and statuettes that looked the worse for wear – that had, in fact, been broken and stuck together. Mrs Stanbridge denied all knowledge of this, as did Nan, but Mrs Stanbridge did point out that Mrs Smith went around with a tube of sticky stuff in her pocket.

Nan had friends in Belfast, and I made it possible for her to take holidays over there. Then one day, without any notice, Mrs Stanbridge told me she was leaving at the weekend. I was hurt and upset. Her excuse was that it was too far for her to travel – although most times Tom took her home in the car.

When Nan came forward saying, Oh, she could see to the house on her own, I pooh-poohed the idea, but she begged me to give her a try. And, as when we first met in the Institution, she worked like no one else would have done. For a time, the house shone – that was, until she felt firmly established again. She came three days a week, and Tom would always take her home with enough food to carry her on until her next visit. One day, she turned to me unexpectedly and said, 'Tom has forgiven me, but you never will, will you, for all the harm I've done you?' So she was aware of how I felt.

As time went on, she picked up her old friends – the doctor and his wife, the estate agent, and others – for was she not a close friend of Mrs Cookson the writer? To all these friends she was dear old Nan, and every Sunday morning they would gather in her flat for a coffee and a smoke and a chat.

There should be some form of operation to cut out charm from characters such as Nan. She had, during this period, a close friend, Sylvia, who had been her officer in the war and had been an actress and artist before that. Her husband had been in the theatre business too, on the artistic side, painting. They were very fond of her.

One day, Sylvia happened to come up to my house and her eyes became riveted on the lovely four-inch Venetian vase piped with gold that was the centrepiece on my study mantelpiece. It was a present that Nan had given me the previous year, but when I saw the look on Sylvia's face, I thought, 'Oh, no, no. She couldn't have; not to a friend.' Sylvia turned to me and smiled wryly, but said nothing. The same thing happened with a soup tureen that Sylvia recognised.

As Nan used to haunt little junk shops and the saleroom basements, I thought she had picked these things up there. But, as I said, she had this trait that, like a dog, she must always bring a present. Although she now knew that friendship couldn't be bought, the idea that she could buy favour through gifts was still with her.

We hadn't been to her flat for some long time and when she didn't turn up one day, we knew something was wrong. We found her, as usual, surrounded by bits and pieces of old furniture and clutter, all dirty, lying in a rumpled bed hardly able to breathe.

When she had been off colour before, I had, when cooking a meal for Tom coming in from school at twenty past twelve, prepared one for her too. I put it under the covers and Tom whisked me in the car to St Leonards nearly three miles away. We left her with a hot meal and a drink, then Tom whisked me back home, after which he gobbled his dinner then made for school again. At different times this had gone on for a week or more. But on this occasion, we saw that she was very ill. We called a doctor in, who said that she had bronchitis and her chest was in such a terrible state that he didn't think she would survive.

What could we do? We got an ambulance and brought her home. And I nursed her for a fortnight, during which time she was near death's door. The doctor told her she must stop smoking if she wanted to go on living. During her convalescence she didn't touch a cigarette – she had got a fright – and when eventually she had to return to the flat it was with great reluctance, and there she started to smoke again.

And so life went on. And just as my mother had caused a great unease in me, so did Nan, but in a different way.

Then came the time when I knew it was an effort for her to do any work at all, and I told her she must give it up. This she did, but I saw to it that she was no worse off.

Oddly enough, she had now moved into the basement flat of the big house on the front at St Leonards that she had once owned, and because I felt she was lonely, we visited her. She still lived among clutter, but it was a tidier clutter because all her friends looked in on a Sunday. One might ask why she had such friends as a doctor and his wife. I think it was because, some years earlier, she had, in her open-handedness, been a friend to the wife when the doctor was doing sea trips. The wife had been left alone with two young boys, and Nan liked playing the Good Samaritan in her own special way. The artists were acquaintances from the camaraderie of the war. Bank managers and solicitors were noticeably absent from the gatherings. At times, she had visits from her Irish friends too and, now and again, from a niece who had been brought up in Nazareth House in Bexhill. Here lies another tale.

It was 1932 when I had first taken a flat, which Nan was sharing with me, when her sister from Ireland arrived on our doorstep with her four young children. What name do you give a woman gambler? I can only think of Nan's sister Maggie as feckless. Apparently, when Nan was in Ireland she ran a stall in the market somewhere and engaged her brother-in-law to ferry things backward and forward to it by means of a handcart. When he was knocked down and killed by some vehicle, she fought the case and got her sister a monthly pension that would provide for her and the children. No sooner had the money come into Maggie's hands but it was gambled away. And so there she was with four mites – I think the eldest boy was about ten. Nan, I recall, scrambled round and got them into rooms. Did I say rooms? A mice- and rat-ridden warren on top of a furniture store in the old town. Nan felt responsible for the lot of them because of how the accident had happened. But I wanted no truck with the dirty individual or her children. When later I took The Hurst and, one Sunday afternoon, the eldest boy wheeled a pram into the drive piled with odds and ends of stuff that his mother wanted me to buy, I hit the ceiling. At that time, I didn't think how dreadful it was for that poor child – the indignity of making him walk from the old town in Hastings right out into the country, uphill all the way, for over two miles pushing that dilapidated pram with those filthy things inside. I understood many years later that that boy had made good and

I was delighted to hear this, but I felt guilty that I hadn't understood his plight. Because mine had been similar in a way when I had been sent to the pawn shop.

Maggie was a thorn in both mine and Nan's sides. And when she ran off with a man and left the children, it was a blessing in disguise, for they were put into Nazareth House to be brought up by the nuns.

But that was not all that happened in those years. After Maggie had decided to descend on her sister, Nan went over to Ireland and brought her mentally deficient child back. This happened shortly after my mother had joined me. Nan was adept at working things out for her own benefit. She could see my mother taking care of the child so everything would be all right. Unfortunately, my mother didn't like children. As for those with mental deficiencies, she had no idea how to handle them as, unlike me, she had never worked with them. Maisie was about seven years old at the time. She liked men and she would follow them if she could get out alone. There was one day when after we found her, Nan thrashed her so unmercifully that I swore I would report her to the NSPCC. I begged her to put the child in care, but she was horrified; she would have none of it.

My mother always swore it was because of this child that she took to drink again. But then she had never stopped – that was just another excuse. The climax came after my mother had returned North and we had guests in the house; Nan was then my housekeeper and she had more time to see to the child, but nobody would bother with her except Nan. And so when Maisie was given more to wandering and having to be brought back by the police, I stood firm and told Nan that she must put her in Nazareth House, where her nieces were. And that's what happened, but only after an awful row.

Later, Maisie was transferred to a home in London: she had a disease that was causing her to swell in all ways. I recall that one Saturday, Nan, Tom and I went up to see her – Nan allowed him to accompany us. I was appalled at the sight of the child; she was like a great big balloon. But she was no longer a child; she was well into her teens. I was saddened, as was Tom. What Nan felt, I don't know.

◆ ◆ ◆

It was about this period that we had an interesting family come to live in the big house across the way. Ours had been a private road at one time, with only the three big houses on it. The first I knew about this family was when I returned from work one day and Mrs Webster and Nan laughingly said, 'You've got posh neighbours across the road.'

'How posh?' I asked.

'Well, the little maid came across and asked if she could have some tea and a cup of sugar.'

'*Never.*'

'It's a fact.'

'What's their name?'

'Captain and Mrs Lee, and there's another captain lives with them called Evans.'

The borrowing became rather frequent during the next few weeks, and I thought it must have been the maid herself doing something on the side. Then I met Mrs Lee.

Mrs Lee was a lady, quiet and reserved. She was of a high-class Irish family who owned linen mills, but her family had cut her off when she married into the army. From what I gathered, the two captains had been cashiered – Evans for having too close an acquaintance with a higher up's wife. He too came from the upper class, and had an allowance that, I learned later, was mostly swallowed up by keeping his two children at public school and supporting his divorced wife. He became a figure in the town noted for driving his little red sports car, looking absolutely spruce and handsome from the waist up, though the soles of his shoes rarely stood inspection.

Yes, here was another charmer, another con man – and indeed he was a con man.

There came the day when they had word that the bums[7] were about to descend on them. It was then that Mrs Lee came across to me, and if ever I felt pity for a woman I did that day. Here was this lady asking me if I would buy her linen so that she would have the fare to Ireland for herself and her child. I hadn't any spare money at the time – although I had guests I was just making ends meet, Nan was seeing to that, but even then, I wouldn't believe she was doing me. But at that woman's request I would have borrowed at that moment to help her. We carted dozens of the most beautiful Irish linen sheets and matching pillowcases and huckaback towels across and I paid her much more than she asked for them. And when later the household things were put up for sale, I bought the carpet that she had had in her drawing room and one or two other things.

The day the house was emptied, Captain Evans came across to me and asked if I would take him as a bed-and-breakfast guest. He could only afford twenty-five shillings a week. I said yes. But from the first day he came into the house, he would sit in the hall as the other guests were going into dinner, so what could one do but say, join us, and for supper too. Moreover, he brought three spaniels with him. He was trying his hand at breeding them.

Smith was seeing that we dealt at the dearest shop in town, and when one day I saw the weekly bill, I went into the kitchen and demanded to know why we should need a dozen jars of double cream and dozens of loaves of bread that we certainly couldn't ever get through. When I made to go into the pantry, Nan Smith yelled at me, 'You're the lady of the house; the kitchen's no place for you. Don't you go in there.'

I went in there. There was a two-foot brown stone jar that the bread was kept in and it was full of mouldy loaves; across the top shelf there

---

7   Bailiffs.

were dozens of jars of cream, some of them green with mould. They had been ordered for Captain Evans's dogs – one of them had had puppies and had to be fed on bread and milk. Such was the mentality of both Mrs Webster and Nan that they hadn't bothered to clear the surplus. There were other things going mouldy pushed at the back of shelves. I was afraid to raise the roof in my own kitchen because Nan's voice could penetrate and there were guests in the house – and she knew I was afraid of rows – but I said most firmly, and in no way that could be misunderstood, that in future I would do the ordering, and would come into the kitchen whenever I liked.

The climax came shortly after this when I realised she wasn't going to give up about Tom. It was then that I took Elphinstone Mount for her and one of the patients volunteered to go with her. He was a Mr Cyril English, who was dying of consumption.

I'd had another TB patient, a beautiful girl called Doris Peacock, whom all men were attracted to. I asked her to leave after I found she was entertaining Captain Evans in her room all night. I had two more elderly guests in rooms nearby, and that kind of thing wasn't to be tolerated – the permissive society hadn't yet arrived.

We had never hit it off but, strangely, although she knew how I felt about her, she wrote to me when we were evacuated to St Albans, when I had the little flat there, and begged me to let her come and live with me. I was pregnant at the time and we only had one bedroom. But even had we had any more, I valued my married life over everything else.

This was the odd thing I found about those years in Hastings – women of all ages and types wanted to come into my life. This became prevalent when I worked in the laundry, where the matron created jealousies among her staff. She once said to me that the only way to keep staff on their toes and to get the work out of them was to put them at each other's throats, and she definitely did that. She certainly wanted to rule my life, and when I wouldn't have it, she created enmity between poor little Nurse Clark, her assistant, and myself, by sending Nurse

Clark over every day to the laundry to inspect the work and talk to my staff. This had never been done before, and I, having been in charge for years, naturally objected to supervisions, especially from someone who knew nothing whatever about the work, and whose person I tried to avoid, for she had skin trouble – particularly around her eyes, poor soul.

The aggravation was fostered by Nan, who was no longer in the laundry but an attendant in the house part of the Institution and in close contact with the matron, who was playing one against the other. All because I wouldn't succumb to her offer of friendship, which I considered suffocating and somewhat unhealthy – and which had already aroused the jealousy of her daughter, who had been brought up from birth in the precincts of the Institution, where free personal service had been afforded her to such an extent that I think she began to imagine that the name of princess – which her mother had bestowed on her – was in fact true.

At times, I was taken for the matron's other daughter. One classic example was the night Mr Wilks, the new assistant master, was invited to tea. I often stayed for tea after the laundry closed – it would have been a daily event if I had allowed it. On this evening, there was to be a staff dance down in the basement of the private house. Such was the matron's attitude towards me that the young man can be forgiven for thinking I was the daughter of the house, for he asked me for the first dance. Then *when* it was finished, he had a rude awakening as Beryl, addressing him in no small voice, said, 'I am the matron's only daughter.' That was that.

Their love affair took on a speed that made her pregnant; then there was a marriage.

At this time, my mother was with me, and we were living in the top two flats of West Hill House and taking summer visitors. The matron asked if Miss Beryl could come down and live with me, and I recall how she said that 'Wilks' would have to pay for her keep. She almost beat me down with her bargaining to a pound a week – this included a private sitting room, three cooked meals a day, her visitors seen to, my mother waiting on her hand and foot and seeing to her through the pregnancy. Unfortunately, the baby was terribly deformed and died within weeks, much to the matron's relief.

Later, when mother and I broke up and I told the matron why – the matron had never liked Kate because she had sinned; this was before her daughter had committed the same offence – her opinion changed somewhat. But apparently, when the matron told Beryl that my mother drank and that was the reason for our break-up, Beryl said that was a lie; she would not believe one word against Mrs McDermott. She was a marvellous woman, and it was a pity that she had to have a daughter like me.

I thought of the nights up in that flat when I'd got Kate off to bed rather than let Beryl discover her altered character when she had a load on.

◆ ◆ ◆

But back to the time when Nan was ill and living in her basement flat. One day, when I was visiting her, she looked at me and said quietly, 'You know I'll haunt you when I die.' I had to get out of the room. When I was going down the stairs, I met Nan's doctor friend and his wife, and they commiserated with me. What was the matter? Was Nan worse? Et cetera, et cetera.

'No,' I said, 'not in health she isn't.' And when I told them what had happened, he laughed and said, 'Oh, but that's Nan with her joking. You should know that by now, if anybody should.' I replied, 'She wasn't joking.' As I left them, I knew they were more sorry for my state of mind than they were for hers.

Then came the day when she was in hospital and very ill, and she asked Tom and me to take her along to her flat, as she wanted to sort out her letters. Tom said, 'But you're too ill, Nan – you can't go along there. You'll never make it; you know you won't.'

'I'll make it all right,' she said. She put her hand on his. 'Just get me to the car, Tom. I want to clear up some things.'

'We can do that for you,' I said.

She looked at me and replied, 'You can't; there's something I want to see to.'

The outcome of this was that the doctor said, 'Well, if she can make it, she can go; there's no use in denying her anything at this stage. She's such a brave woman, a fine character.'

Dear, dear, dear, what charm does.

So we got her to the flat. I had tidied things up as much as I could, and I had cooked a dinner – in the flat – for her two Irish friends whom she had written to and told they could have whatever they wanted with regards to furniture et cetera. They were like vultures and had already put their stamp on what they would take back to Ireland. And it was amazing the stuff that they had packed up: box and parcel on top of parcel. How they managed it on the railway and the boat, I don't know, but they were determined to take all they could carry or pull.

Anyway, there she was, sitting surrounded by literally hundreds and hundreds of letters, throwing them aside in bundles for burning as she joked with the two women.

Becoming very tired, she suddenly said, 'They can all be burned. I've got what I want.' This was a small woven pouch, which looked as if it held about three or four papers or letters. When she had first come into the flat, she had taken this from a drawer and put it into her bag.

She was on the point of exhaustion when we got her into the car, and when she was once more in the hospital bed, she looked up at us and said, 'That's that then.' She went on to explain what money she had coming from insurance and the few debts that she owed, I said to her, 'Don't worry, Nan, about that.' I lied as I went on, 'It will be a long time before that has to be seen to.' She lay back and looked at me. It was a soft look that I remembered from the early days before she had become vicious – or had she always been vicious? I was soon to have the answer to this.

It was during the period when I was in demand to give talks here and there across the country, which was very gratifying. As long as I could get over the journey, or wasn't forced to leave the stage because of a bleeding – which ironically happened once when I was speaking at a nurse's conference – I liked what I called platform work. The suggestions I got from the medical ladies as to the best way to stop the bleeding were amusing – one even said that her granny always found it helpful to put a key down her back.

I had also been on television a number of times. It's odd the things that one remains proud of. In my case, it was a letter from The Independent Television in Newcastle. I had been asked to appear on a programme; it was quite a big do: a half-hour talk then questions from the selected audience. While I was up there I was giving a talk in Newcastle. I'd waived my fee and said I would just take my expenses, as that particular society wasn't very well off – I gave all my fees to charity, mostly to the RSPCA and the NSPCC. So when I got an expense form from the Independent Television, I said I wouldn't be charging any as I had been paid by the society to whom I had given a talk. I got a letter from the head of the department saying that it was the first time he had known anyone to refuse their expenses, and he thanked me for a new experience.

Pride, I suppose, in my honesty, but it was justified, I think, because even today I am shocked at what people will put down as expenses on their accounts. But I'm getting away from the point, and yet not, because I was due to do this programme and talk the weekend that Nan was actually dying.

We had sat with her most of the week. She was on oxygen, and when the day came that I was due to travel North, I said to Tom, 'I can't go.' 'You must,' he said. 'You can do no good here. You've gone through enough, and you can't help her anymore.'

I was in a state. I forgot all that had happened between us: all the years of misery she had put me through, and all the lies she had told about me. How she had tried to blacken Tom's character. I forgot the suicide threats that had been her means of blackmailing me for years. I forgot everything except my pity for her. I held her hands, looked deep into her shrunken face and said, 'Goodbye, Nan.' And she smiled at me. I was to remember that smile. How could it be soft, kindly, loving? When I left her, I was blinded with tears.

Tom told me later that once I had left the room, she said, 'Now I can die, Tom.' He stayed with her, holding her hand until, late that night, she died. But before she went, she said to him, 'You'll see to my private things, won't you? In that cupboard there is a pouch with some letters in it, and you already know about my bills and whatever arrangements are to follow . . .'

I was staying at my cousin's. Tom phoned me there the following morning – this would be the Friday – and told me she was still alive. He did not want me to be disturbed more than I was until I had done the television programme and my talk.

On the Sunday morning, he phoned and told me she had died on the Thursday after I'd left. But when I said I was coming straight home for the funeral, he became unusually emphatic and said, No, I must not come.

Why?

Just because I would be much more distressed than I was – I had to stay there and take it easy for the next few days. She'd be buried on Tuesday.

I thought this odd, but realised there was nothing I could do for her now if I did return home. Yet, as I said to him, her friends would think it very strange if I wasn't at her funeral, and his reply to this was, 'Let them . . .'

He met me at the station on the Wednesday evening, and he had hardly said hello when I started telling him how guilty I felt for not being at her funeral. I should have been there; it was the least I could do et cetera, et cetera. When we got into the house, he said, 'Sit yourself down and look at these.' He pushed towards me the hand-woven pouch, saying, 'The sister handed me her private belongings. She'd likely gone through them, *and remember Nan made that special journey* when she was dying to pluck up these letters; they were all she wanted from her house.'

There were three letters in the pouch. As I took the first one out of the envelope, I recognised my own handwriting. It began, 'Dearest Nan, of course I will have you as a friend and openly. You came into my life when I was lonely and lost and I'm going to the office in the morning to tell the matron that we are friends. She can't do anything about it. I'm at liberty to choose my own friends. Fortunately, I don't live in.'

On and on in the same vein. I recalled this was the answer I wrote to her letter in which she asked me if we could be friends.

It was no light thing I was doing in openly declaring my friendship with a scrubber in the laundry. I had a position to uphold, and everyone knew that she had been a scrubber on the wards before she had been sent to the laundry. I could understand her keeping this letter. I looked at Tom. He nodded towards the second one, which was in a foreign envelope; I opened it and read.

Dear Paddy,[8]
We are so very sorry for you, mama is distressed, she knows how you feel . . . and is distressed for you about Miss Mac and her new man. You have put up with all her men and doings and now she has thrown you out for a boy, so young a schoolmaster, he but twenty-four

---

8   'Paddy' was a nickname for Nan.

years old and she over thirty. We know how you feel
and about all her men, it is wicked. And he does not
know about her men, the one who came to the house
early in the morning at seven to take her to work or
business and is to divorce his wife. And her other men
who let her have furniture cheap . . .

On and on it went, and I couldn't believe what I was reading. This
letter was from the fifteen-year-old son of a French woman who had
holidayed at The Hurst some years previously, before I had met Tom.
I must explain about her. She had been recommended by some other
French people who had stayed with us some time previously. She was
small, fat and in her forties, but smartly dressed and came, I understood, from a very high-class Parisian family. So much so that she would
have nothing to do with the nice French couple who were staying with
us at the same time because they were merely school teachers from the
poor end of Paris.

It was our first season in The Hurst. My mother was doing the
cooking and enjoying herself thoroughly with her practical jokes on
the guests, which they too seemed to enjoy, except when she gave them
a box for lunch, which when opened proved to be full of pan scrubs,
corks, string, bobbins and such. She always thought her tricks were very
clever. Practical jokers are the only people who get pleasure out of their
jokes; the recipients have to grin and bear it so as not to be classed as
spoilsports.

At the time I am speaking of, we had about fifteen guests, and in
the evening they would gather in the drawing room and have a sing-
song. Everybody seemed very happy, except the little French woman
who never joined in but sat aloof, a pained look on her face, even while
her son sang and danced in the hall with the other guests – the hall in
The Hurst provided a lovely dance floor.

Madame Blaut was booked to stay for a month. In the second week, I became concerned for her; she seemed unhappy. One night as she was going to bed, I met her on the landing and asked if there was anything I could do for her.

She shook her head and then said, 'I feel very lonely and lost here; no one is friendly.'

'But, madame, everyone feels friendly towards you and they want you to join in; it's only that they don't speak French and you rarely speak in English to them. Oh, my dear, please don't be sad.' At that, I leaned forward and kissed her on the cheek. I wasn't given to kissing, but she looked so sad and lost. 'You will feel better next week when your husband arrives,' I said.

'You will be my friend?'

'Yes, of course, of course.'

That was the beginning. The following night at five o'clock when I came out of the Institution's gates, there she was waiting for me. I thought, how nice and how clever I was to have broken through her reserve. I made her laugh most of the way home.

But the next morning, there she was ready to accompany me to work, and so it went on. She haunted me and objected to other people taking up my time. When her husband arrived, she had him meet me at the gates too, but she herself accompanied me to work.

The husband was a very nice man, but he treated her as if she was a doll – a pretty little doll, or a child. He patted her bottom, he patted her cheek, he kissed her and ooh, lalahed her, saying, 'My petite dear' or 'My little girlie'. He was a wealthy businessman and apparently had always indulged her.

He only stayed a week and she stayed on an extra week, and would have been there yet if I hadn't promised to visit them in Paris. When the subject was first broached, I made the excuse that I couldn't afford such a trip, and thought that was that.

On the Sunday when I had put her on the boat at Dover, I heaved a great sigh and thought, 'Thank God.' And asked again of Him, 'Why is it that women want to latch on to me?' I had become afraid of this because it had happened frequently over the years. I asked myself, 'Is there something wrong with me?' But I could find no answer. I saw myself as a pretty normal being, both physically and mentally, and a suffering one because my mother at the time was at her worst.

The climax with my mother happened one Christmas Day when Davie [Kate's husband] was home from sea. We had one paying guest staying with us – a Miss Sayers, whose sister would also be coming to dinner that day. Kate had started on the whisky early in the morning. I can recall the fear that was in me as I approached her in the pantry, saying softly, pleadingly, 'Don't touch any more until after they've gone, will you not?' I asked as a child might. I got a bawling scream for an answer. It had never passed her lips, but she would show me. And she did show me. She went to the sideboard and she took out numerous bottles and mixed them and threw a glass filled with the whisky at me. Then, crying loudly, she picked up a pair of Davie's heavy stoke-hole boots and levelled them at my head. It was a Christmas Day I'll never forget. In the middle of the silent dinner, she rushed away upstairs crying and screaming.

I remember Miss Sayers was so kind. She said she understood perfectly, as she had looked after an aunt with the same trouble for years. She left the next week. And there I was alone with Kate. I told her it couldn't go on; in fact, at that period I was near finishing it myself. Nan had left the house by then and gone down to the flats that I was still having to pay twenty-five shillings a week for as I had leased them for three years, and we were only in them a year before we moved into The Hurst.

How did I come through that time? Why didn't I have a breakdown then? I'd gone through enough to send ten people mad.

When Kate, solid and sober, faced up to the fact that I couldn't endure any more, she went on her knees to me and begged me to let her stay. My God! That was a dreadful time; dreadful to see a mother going on her knees and pleading with her daughter. What could I do? 'All right,' I said. 'If you promise to give up the spirit.' I told her I didn't mind her having the beer, and would see that she got some every day.

So from then on, I would dash from the laundry at twelve o'clock to the outdoor beer shop on the road opposite, buy a pint bottle of beer, then make another dash across the allotments. After giving it to her and having a cup of tea, there was no time for a meal, even if I could have eaten it. My dinner was an apple.

This went on for a month until I began to return home to a darkened house and there she would be, supposedly with a sick headache, sleeping it off upstairs. I knew I could stand little more, so I gave her the option: either she would go or I would walk out and the house would be sold. She went, but she had to have a big house like mine.

It was around this time that Madame Blaut sent me the fare to come to Paris, and I gladly went. They all seemed delighted to see me, and the husband took us all to lunch and to the opera on the Saturday night; I recall it was *Hérodiade*.

On the Sunday, we had lunch with Madame Blaut's parents, very high-ups who treated me with courtesy, but no doubt wondered why their daughter had made friends with this English girl.

Nan Smith had been much in evidence at The Hurst during Madame Blaut's stay, and as usual had been very entertaining and made friends with a number of the guests. Moreover, during our third year at The Hurst, there was the great con man Captain Evans – a charmer in his own right – so our guests were always entertained and wanted to come back.

On the return journey from France, there was a terrific storm and I became so sea sick that I was ill for two days. I had tried to sever all connection with my mother and I know she was spreading the most atrocious lies about me from Nan. Whatever my mother says or does – or which company she decides to keep is no longer any concern of mine.

She had a paying guest, a master at the grammar school, and Davie was working on a boat sailing between Newcastle and London. So I thought she was all right money-wise. I was in bed with a bad bout of bleeding when I got a letter from her to say that the schoolmaster had left but she had got another one, a young man, a maths master, and she wanted to see me particularly. Would I come down?

It was days later when I was able to go. I've told the story of my first seeing Tom and his first glimpse of me, and that was that.

With regard to the previous schoolmaster, I heard from him later that year when things had come to another head and my mother had promised to return North if I would settle up her debts. I was only managing to scrape along at that time by keeping my job and trying to run the guest house on the side with the questionable assistance of Nan and Mrs Webster. But I called a halt to paying any more of her debts when the schoolmaster wrote and asked me if I would please send him the money she had borrowed from him. I had been brought low when I had to accompany Davie to the owners of the house next door and ask them to free her from the three-year lease.

Oh dear me, why is all this flooding back? Still, it hasn't been told and need never be told, but I feel I must talk about it, and yet I am not telling all because I can hardly believe myself the things I suffered from her hands and Nan Smith's without retaliating and sending them both to hell years ago. People wouldn't believe that the world-famous novelist Catherine Cookson, or Miss Mac as I was then, would put up with what both of them made me suffer.

But back to reading the letter from the French boy . . .

I looked up at Tom, and he put out his hand and laid it on mine, then I continued to read about all these men that I'd gone through in my life.

To begin with I used to go to three different second-hand shops, Reeves', Cracknell's and Papworth's, all in the old town. I'd put a shilling a week off this or two shillings off that. I got most of my Mappin and Webb silver from Mr Cracknell. From Mr Reeves I bought my first chair, and I still have it. From Mr Papworth, an old piano and an oak dining room suite that I bought when I first took the flats in 1932, and which served me well until we left the South in 1976.

When I first took The Hurst, Mr Cracknell said to me, 'I've got some beautiful curtains that were in an Embassy in Paris; they had just been put up when the husband was ordered home, and the wife brought them with her, but they didn't fit the windows of their new house. They would fit yours.' He said, 'I'm collecting them tomorrow, and I'll drop them in and you can have a look at them.'

I had a look at them; they were magnificent: six large pairs of golden padded silk with great rope tassels. I had to have them. 'How much?' I said.

'Five pounds.'

Oh dear me, five pounds; it was a lot of money, but I realised they were worth fifty times that.

I took them, and they were a delight to me for years. The edges faded, but forty years later I put them in a sale and was pleased to see a woman grab them with as much delight as I had done when I first saw them, and for eight times what I had paid for them forty years earlier.

So those were the men in my life that the French boy was referring to. And there was another; he had a new furniture shop and a second-hand one on the upper floor. I bought old-fashioned bedroom suites from him to help fill up the six main bedrooms and four attics in The Hurst. I also bought some new curtain material, and he came and measured the amount I would need. He offered to have them sewn for me, but I couldn't afford it, so I sat up at night and until early in the morning sewing away on yards and yards of material.

Then there was John Cole, whom I have mentioned; poor John, who took his own life. He visited the house; our mutual interest was old furniture: antiques in his case, large stuff that I could buy cheap in mine.

Speaking of the antique dealers, I was amazed when one of them stopped speaking to me after the first time he saw me in a sale room. He had lost a good customer.

Then there was the assistant master at the Institution who came to tea. He was engaged at the time.

I had told Nan of the two men I had met during my first two years in Hastings. One had introduced me to music at the White Rock. I had thought he was single until he told me he had been to see his wife with regard to getting a divorce and marrying me . . . He nearly disappeared over the cliff on imparting that. Married men were a menace to me. The second one who would have married me – if I would have had him – decided against it because of my strong objection to premarital relations. Then there was the young man who came from The Sun Life of Canada Company to see me because I was putting up the premium. He took me and my musical friend to Eastbourne for dinner.

There they all were in this letter, referred to as 'my men'. On and on, even the casuals from the road looking for work.

The third letter was hardly worth mentioning. I didn't see the point in it. It was from an officer in the First World War. Nan had been in the Women's Army, and this letter was from an officer thanking her for her offer of friendship, but saying that under the circumstances it wouldn't work, or words to that effect.

If Tom hadn't been the man he was, if he hadn't known of her jealousy and the lies she had told about him, he would have undoubtedly questioned the significance of what was implied in these letters. The question was, what on earth had she written to Madame Blaut about me that had made that boy write in these terms?

What followed next was something that I hope I will never experience in my life again, for there arose in me a terrifying feeling: a white-hot rage. It made me want to smash something, tear at something. I felt like an animal, chained, but facing a corpse that I wanted to render into shreds. The feeling was the embodiment of a dreadful hate. They say love is the strongest emotion. Oh no, not by fathoms or miles can it touch real hate. I walked about the house like a madwoman, talking all the time.

'I've looked after her for years. She's evil. Evil. She got us to take her to that flat just to get those letters. She left them for you to open. She wanted to break us up; she was determined to separate us from the grave. Don't you understand?'

Yes, yes, he understood. He understood it more than I did or ever will that evil can hide itself as hers had done for years. That her jealousy had fed on it. 'But why? Why?' I kept asking myself. Because she had got me. Tom in his kindness and compassion wouldn't have minded her living with us. He didn't know that even before I had met him I would have been glad of any excuse to break the friendship, for we had nothing in common. She was an ignorant woman, unable to learn; all she had was her charm, and of course her generosity that was in the main provided by others – namely myself at that time.

In the next few days, I started to write down how I felt about her, bits here and there, pouring out this hate. I felt a changed being.

At the end of a week, I felt ill, and it came to me that her intentions were bearing fruit: if not in the way she had first intended, in another way that was just as effective, for she was destroying me. She said she would haunt me and she was.

I began to reason, and endeavoured to think quietly. Then I sat down and spoke to her. 'No, Nan, no. You're not going to do it. Hate can destroy; you know that. It destroyed you, but you're not going to destroy me through it. You're out of my life now, and I'm going to put you out of my mind. You have lost, do you hear? What you planned, lying there on your sickbed, Tom and me daily by your side caring for you, has fallen flat. It is as nothing. In fact, it has only helped to develop the great bond of love that is between us. Nothing or no one can separate us – that can only come by death. And if I ever pray again, it'll be that in the long hereafter, I will never have to see the shadow of you.'

The hate left me, but I could not forgive or forget. I tried to understand the motives that made her do it, but couldn't find an answer. Evil such as hers didn't come out of love. Real love could not breed the ruin of another's life. Real love could not pretend a friendship for us both as she had done for years and years.

Looking back, I realised that all along I had feared her, even though I did not know what I had to fear from her.

Fear had filled my life. My young days had been lived in fear. I feared Kate; oh yes, I had to be careful what I said to Kate. I feared upsetting her, making her mad. Then I feared because I had denied God. Fear! Fear!

Some time ago, when I knew that my mind and spirit were not at peace, I thought, 'It is because I can't forgive.' I couldn't forgive Hannah McDermott for trying to take the only good thing I valued in those early days in Harton – which was my good name, even if it was my step-grandfather's.

I couldn't forgive Jim Daly [the author does not explain who this is] for using me for over two years as a salve on the wound of his broken engagement, which I knew nothing about in the beginning. *And I couldn't forgive Nan Smith.* Perhaps this was why I hadn't real peace of mind and spirit. I must forgive them. So I tried. I tried over different periods of time. Now I don't know whether I've forgiven them or not. I know that I cannot forget. It's utter nonsense, this talking of forgiving and forgetting – scars remain, mental or physical. The mental have the more impact. Yet, in spite of this, I have gained a measure of peace of mind and spirit. As I said, I can face up to the fact of death and, were there a Maker, of meeting Him. I have learned to devalue possessions and to ignore so-called fame. So, as I see it, I am progressing slowly but surely towards the peace of mind that surpasseth all understanding.

Before I get off this subject, I must explain about my other men – the casuals from the Institution. Even Madame Blaut questioned me about one of these.

During the late 1920s and early 1930s, the roads were full, not of the ordinary professional tramp, but of young and middle-aged men looking for work; travelling mostly from the North and Wales towards the South. Some of them were decently dressed and well spoken, and here and there was a well-educated one. Ninety-five per cent of them were looking for work – any kind of work.

When we first took The Hurst, my mother said, 'That garden needs a man on it.' But we hadn't the money to pay for a gardener. Every night in the summer when I wasn't sewing at those curtains or something else, I'd be in the garden, swatting or mowing. She said to me, 'Couldn't you get one of the lads that are sent over to the laundry to come and do a few hours? I could always feed them and we could give them a few shillings?'

It was an idea. So when a young fellow in his early twenties, quiet-looking and definitely a working lad, was sent over to me, together with another three, to do wash house work – such as pulling heavy bogies and carrying sacks of dirty linen – I said to him, 'Would you like a few hours' work?'

'Oh yes, miss,' he said. 'Oh yes.' So I gave him the address and told him to go to the house the next morning. I said, 'I can't give you more than five shillings, but you'll get three good meals and it'll set you on your way.'

'Thank you very much, miss. Thank you, indeed.'

He said his name was Henry. Mam liked Henry. More so when she realised he had been to sea, but as they were laying up boats he could not get set on again. 'How would it be,' she said, 'if we keep him on for a time, give him pocket money of ten shillings a week' – and ten shillings was ten shillings in those days – 'and,' as she put it, 'get some work out of him and that garden tidied up?'

So Henry was engaged. He had no conversation. To me, it was, 'Yes, miss,' and 'No, miss.' He slept long hours, going to bed at eight at night and was never up when I left the house at half past seven in the morning. He ate like a ravenous horse – and like a horse, he shied at the thing called work.

Having my suspicions how Henry spent his time, I didn't go straight into the house one night as I returned from work. I also made it my business to get home a little earlier by taking the bus for half the journey. The garden looked much as I had left it in the morning, and of course it was, because there, curled into a nice ball under the rhododendron bushes fast asleep, was Henry.

Henry was told to mend his ways or else.

He didn't wait for or else; he took his little bundle and walked out the next day without saying goodbye to Mam. That was the first one.

The second one was Gentleman John. He was tall, good-looking and well dressed. He spoke well too, but it was through copying, not through education, and like Kate, he was a bit of a Mrs Malaprop. That didn't matter, for the house was full of summer visitors and Kate was saying, 'If we could get a young fellow to help with that hall floor . . .' The hall floor was polished with a foot-square bumper and there was a knack in swinging it from side to side. I learned it, but the maid we had was too refined for such lowly work. 'A man who'll turn his hand to anything,' Mam said, 'is what's needed.' So, when out of the blue Gentleman John appeared at my office door before returning to the house to enjoy his bread, cheese and soup meal, and without any prelim said, 'I'm looking for employment, temporarily. I understand you are in need of summer help at your house at the moment . . .'

How did he know? Oh yes, of course, I had mentioned something like this to Mrs Beecham, my assistant, and she, likely wanting to help this smart, attractive man – he wasn't a young fellow; he was well into his thirties, nearing forty I should say – had given him the tip.

'We only need someone for a month to six weeks,' I said. 'And you can be called upon to do all odd jobs, and the pay is only fifteen shillings a week and what tips you can get.'

'That will suit me very well. I suppose you'll want me to start immediately.'

'Yes.'

He started immediately and proved to be an all-round man in more ways than one. He took in the situation with my mother and me immediately. He saw her weakness. He had imagined he'd summed me up too. I was a go-ahead young woman carrying on two businesses.

He made himself indispensable. He and Nan hit it off immediately – their charm linked. He also turned out to be a surprisingly good dancer and was very much in demand with the young guests.

There was something about him that worried me, though, and I was worried enough about Mam at the same time. She was too busy to get out, yet there was that look on her face that I dreaded. Her spirits were too high. She made herself the centre of notice, pushing herself into the company and acting the goat, to my deep embarrassment. This was always the result of whisky.

She was getting it from somewhere, but where? I took our new assistant aside and said, 'Has my mother ever asked you to bring spirits in for her?'

He looked at me solemnly and shook his head and said, 'No.'

'Will you promise me something?'

'Yes, anything in the world, Miss Mac.'

I passed over the familiarity of his tone and said, 'Promise me you'll never bring spirits in, no matter how she begs? Please, will you promise me that?'

'Yes, of course I will, Miss Mac.'

He was another incarnate of Smith – he could look you in the face tenderly as he lied. He had been supplying her with whisky at the rate of a bottle every two days since he had first come into the house.

After he had been there three weeks, it was almost as if he had been there three years. He had settled in so well and everybody liked him – he was so obliging. But I was still worried about him.

One night after the guests had departed to their rooms and I'd helped to clear up the kitchen, and Kate had taken her swollen legs and her bottle to bed with her, I went out into the warm night just to be by myself for a few minutes. I stood leaning on the gate, looking into the road and asking myself, 'What of the future?' In spite of all the people round me for sixteen hours of the day or more, I was lonely and lost inside.

I didn't become aware of the gentleman until he said, 'It's a lovely night, isn't it?'

He too leaned on the gate, and as he did he told me that he had never felt so settled in his life before. That he had the idea that he might stick around Hastings, get a job – there were big houses on the outskirts, and one or two of them had been turned into hotels. He would apply for a waiter's post or, with a bit of luck, a butler or gardener-chauffeur. He could turn his hand to most things.

There was something in his tone that put me on my guard.

The following night when I got in, Kate seemed mostly her sober self and, taking me aside, she said, 'There's nothing growing atween you and him, is there?'

'You mean . . . ?'

'Yes, you know who I mean.'

When I didn't answer but stared at her, she said, 'My God! Davie would go mad if you married anybody like that.'

Davie would go mad? Davie was a quiet fellow who hardly ever opened his mouth; she had all the say. Davie would go mad, indeed. It was she who would go mad. Her stay would be gone. And it came

161

to me in that moment that I was her stay, her security, and always had been. I said to her now, 'What's put that into your head?'

'Well, there's been talk among the guests, and somebody saw you and him at the gate last night together. And he's been throwing his weight about in that direction. Let me tell you something – he could be a dangerous man, and he's a liar too.'

Looking at her straight in the face, I said, 'Aren't we all?' I recall she turned from me saying, 'Something'll have to be done.'

What with the clinging French lady, Nan and her possessiveness, Mam and her drinking, and now Gentleman John, not counting the worry of money – for even with the house full for months past, I didn't seem to be making any profit – everything seemed to be going on food, laundry, electric bills, coal and what have you, and Nan was only giving me half what I expected to pay for our food while taking from me with both hands. Whisky was never cheap, and of course Mam would give Gentleman John a good backhander for getting it on the sly for her.

Then Nan came to me and said, 'You'd better do something about that fellow; he's getting too big for his boots. What if I tell him you're engaged to be married to a Northern chap and that he's someone of importance – legal like. Something like that – say a solicitor?'

'All right,' I said. 'You can do, but you're all barking up the wrong tree.' They weren't barking up the wrong tree, and I knew it.

So Nan supposedly let the cat out of the bag about my engagement to this big nob in the North. The result of this was that I was confronted by a very stiff-faced employee, a gentleman who could turn his hand to anything. Was it true what he heard, that I was engaged to a man in the North?

I sighed as I said, 'Yes, it was.'

What was his name and profession?

Why shouldn't I give the name of a man I knew who had been very fond of me in my teenage years? He was fifteen years older than me and he lived in a terrace in the New Buildings, and at one time, in a girlish way when I was about fifteen, I'd imagined I was in love with him. I was searching at that time for a father figure. I said, 'His name is John Dyer and he's a solicitor.' He wasn't.

'Oh, well,' he said, 'that won't stop me from sticking around.'

Perhaps it was mentioning his name, but some time later, when I was feeling lonely and lost and imagining that I would never fall in love again, but with the need on me to marry and have children, I wrote to this old friend, as I thought of him, and a correspondence sprang up that ended in him coming for a week's holiday. It was disastrous. The first sight of him told me I had done a wrong thing in building up his hopes. I was then twenty-nine, and he in his middle forties and so changed and settled in his bachelor ways. But we parted friends, and I was left more lonely than ever and feeling sure now that love would never again enter my life, for I was incapable of the feeling, and thought that it had been burned out of me in my late teens.

What happened to Gentleman John?

Well, what he did at the end was most uncharacteristic. Mam had asked him to take an order down to our grocer in the town, and he didn't come back. That afternoon, the grocer phoned to say that something had been troubling him. Had my manservant come back? Mam replied, 'No.' Then he told her that the man had called with the order and said that he had inadvertently come out without his wallet and he had to pick up one or two things for the house, and could he have the loan of two pounds until this afternoon when he would be coming in again? Well, he hadn't returned, and the grocer recalled that the man had a case with him, as if he was about to take a journey rather than go on more errands.

I later told him to put the two pounds on my bill, then asked myself, 'Why on earth had the man to make a thief of himself for two pounds? He could have asked me for twice that much and I would have advanced it, and he could have walked out then.'

Some weeks later, I had a letter from a lady who had stayed at the house two or three times before with her younger sister – younger, but who could still earn the title of maiden lady – and she was very surprised when they had a visitor. Who should it be, but Mr John, who said he was resident now in London, and would count it a favour if he could call on them from time to time. She added that his old-fashioned courtesy didn't cut any ice with her as she had never liked the man and had lied to him politely, saying that they were going away for an extended holiday.

I wonder what became of him?

Well, that was the second of my lame dogs. The third turned out to be a pair, and their stay ended much more dramatically.

By this time, my mother was back in the North and the house was being run by Nan as the supposed nurse-housekeeper with Mrs Webster as the cook, for I had acquired Miss Pansy Wilcox, an epileptic, and also a mentally affected young girl who was the daughter of a big businessman in the town. I had decided to see to the garden myself because of my past experience with gentlemen help from the Institution. What we needed were paths, and I had an idea of making a fishpond on a rise at the edge of the lawn. To this end, I went to watch some men making cement for the new houses in the next road. 'Three in one,' they said, and laughed when I told them I was going to make fancy-coloured bricks. So, what I did was to buy pounds of yellow, red and blue ochre, mix up some cement, divide it into batches, tint it with the colours, then fill up wood squares and diamonds that I'd made out of boxes. I would do this in the evening. The following morning when partly set, I would knock off the wood and leave the bricks to dry. When I had batches of twenty, I laid them in a big circle around the hole I had dug for the pool. I must say that I did have help with the pool: the husband of one of my workers came up two Sundays to give me a hand. I waited for him on the third Sunday, but he didn't come. His wife said he wasn't well. My assistant told me that he said he wasn't going up there again because I worked like a navvy, as his wife only too truly knew.

There came a day when two young lads – one about eighteen, the other nineteen – were sent to me from the casual ward to do wash house work. They looked so young, and I thought it was terrible that they should be on the road. So when they asked if I could give them a job up at my house – they heard I had a big garden – I sighed and said, 'All right.' What could go wrong with two young lads? But I told them, 'Only for a week.' And I could only give them a pound, together with their board and lodgings. They thanked me warmly and said it would be a godsend to get off the road for a week.

They worked so hard and so well in that week that Nan said, 'Keep them on for a while longer and have the outhouse and garden cleared up and tidy for the winter.'

The following week on the Friday night, when I handed them a pound, the older one said, 'Bobbie's trousers are dropping to bits. I'm going down into the town to get him a new pair.' He went down into the town with the pound and didn't come back. We couldn't believe it. There was the other lad, who I realised was a weak character, but with hardly a rag to his back, and his pal had scarpered with the wages. What could I do? I couldn't send the lad packing.

The other one dared to return on the Monday evening saying he was sorry he had been tempted and blew the pound. I told him to get on his way and he said, 'All right, but don't take it out on Bobbie; he hasn't done anything.'

So Bobbie stayed and became the pet of Mrs Webster. I'd find her lying on the couch in the kitchen, the boy stroking her wiry hair – it used to stand up as if she was in constant fright from her domed forehead. She was a weird-looking woman altogether. She said the boy put her in mind of the son she had lost. She'd never had a son in her life, or a daughter. All she had ever given birth to was imagination, but it appeared to me that she wanted sex so much she didn't care who it'd be with. She then accused the man next door of tackling her in the dark passage that led down between the houses. The man was a very respectable individual and he would have been badly in need of sex to take her on. Anyway, there was Bobbie being pampered by this old, weird woman and his sex instincts brought to blood heat by a young maid I had engaged – the daughter of one of my staff. She was the kind of simpering girl that would always cause trouble among trousers, even if they were hanging on the line.

In the house at that time there was Nan Smith, Mrs Webster, this girl, the young fellow, the two permanent patients and Captain Evans to see to, besides a few weekly guests. These last were mostly people who had been there before, and I knew they weren't satisfied with the way the house was run at the present.

Each year, I took my holiday at the height of the season so I could see to things and I look back on that period as if I were two different people. One, the businesswoman who took pride in her efficiency and getting the best out of labour, combined with the guest-house proprietress. On the other hand, there was this fear-ridden, worrying and trusting individual. So trusting that I left the cash box in one of the linen cupboards on the landing – there were no locks to these cupboards, nor yet on the bedroom doors – and, near the cash box was another, into which went the tips that were to be shared out at the end of the season.

It was twelve o'clock one day when the maid appeared in the laundry; she was gasping, having run all the way from the house. It seemed that the young fellow had smashed one of a pair of statues and gone off with the cash box.

The two statues had stood on pedestals at each side of the big window in the drawing room. I had bought them when I first took my little flat – they were beautiful figures and I loved them.

When I got home, the house was in uproar. I called in the police and they found the boy's old jacket hanging in the wine cellar and in it was a note addressed to me. It stated what he thought about me and went on to say that if there had been more money to take, he would have taken it.

He had been asked to clean the drawing-room windows and his answer had been to smash the statue, apparently because he knew it was something that I valued.

Of course, all the staff in the laundry were agog. In fact, the staff in the whole Institution were agog and were enjoying the fact that the northerner had been done.

The police couldn't trace the boy and so the matter seemed to drop until three or four months later when one of my girls came into the office and said, 'I think you should know, Miss Mac, that those two fellows have come back into the casual ward, the porter's just said.'

I stared at her dumbfounded. I couldn't believe it. That they had dared to come into the Institution knowing that likely they would be sent to the laundry and would have to face me. I recall what the elder one said to me the night he returned to confess that he had spent the pound. Just before he departed, he had grinned at me and said, 'You know you ask for this 'cos you're a soft touch. All the stiff Miss Mac stuff is only a coatin'.'

Now they were going to have a laugh on the soft touch and get the Institution buzzing with their daring.

The girl's name was Violet Tuppenny. I did not even answer her, but walked straight past her, down to the laundry, through the wash house – all eyes on me – into the boiler room, where there was a phone, and immediately rang the police and told them the man who had robbed me had come into the casual ward with his pal.

Within half an hour he was picked up and taken to the police station. They couldn't do anything with the older fellow because he hadn't robbed me, only stolen his pal's wages. He did not show his face in the laundry the next day, and I understood he did a bunk without doing his day's chores.

When the case came up a fortnight later, I went to the court and watched the clerk hand the magistrate the note that the prisoner, as he was then, had left for me. The magistrate made a remark to the effect that this was the reward people received for showing kindness and consideration to a tramp. As they took him from the court, he turned and looked at me: his face was livid and he no longer looked a young boy. Later, the policeman told me he said he didn't mind if they sent him to prison, but he dreaded being sent to Borstal. Apparently, he had been there before. I also learned that he had been thrown out of his home by his father, who had a small fishing boat of some kind down in the West Country.

Anyway, the attitude in the Institution towards me changed. They wouldn't attempt to laugh up their sleeves at me again. Clearly, that Miss McMullen was as strong as she appeared to be and afraid of no one. Oh, if only they had known what Miss McMullen had been going through. Fear was my bed companion. Anyway, that was the last, I told myself. No more helping lame dogs; never again.

What!

Well, the fourth one didn't happen in the same way, and turned out to be much more pleasant.

We knew an old lady who ran a little farm together with her daughter and the help of various slightly mentally defective young men. The farm was on the outskirts of the town and I had, at times, dropped in and had a chat with Mrs Burgess. She had been upset for me over the court case and had suggested that I take on a boy similar to the ones she had.

'Oh no,' I said. 'Oh no, I'm dealing with that kind all day. Anyway, I have an epileptic and a mental one in the house already . . .' With regards to terming the second patient mental, her parents wouldn't have that name applied to her, oh no. She had only gone slightly odd because she wouldn't eat, was their version of her condition.

At the time, besides the two patients and, of course, the sponger Captain Evans, there was Miss Doris Peacock, Tom and a Miss Rouyl.

Looking back, I'm amazed how people with money could beat you down to the last penny. Strangely, although I saved every penny, I never could haggle with people over money, so I was always the loser in that way. I recall Miss Rouyl's brother, an elderly gentleman, coming to the house to ask if I could take her.

Was she an invalid?

Oh no, she needed only slight attention; she suffered from a little arthritis. He himself travelled and he wanted to see her settled in a comfortable home before he went on his next journey – I didn't know his journeys were from one comfortable hotel to another, but still in this country.

The fee would be two pounds ten a week.

Oh, he couldn't afford that. No, no, not for a long-time stay, and he promised me that. What about two pounds?

So Miss Rouyl came – he didn't accompany her, as he had gone on one of his journeys – and she had to be lifted out of the taxi with the help of two people and into the study that had been turned into a bedroom for her. Her brother had admitted that she couldn't make the stairs. What he didn't admit was she couldn't make anything with regard to helping herself. She had to be lifted into bed and out, bathed, her meals brought to her room, and demanded the full-time attention of a nurse in the form of Nan. All for two pounds a week.

I'll say this for her, she had a sweet nature. She also had money that her brother saw to, and he had the nerve to come and stay weekends – at a reduced rate, of course. I recall one weekend when my cousins, Jack and Alec, were staying with me for a day or so. They were both very presentable young men. Jack was in the navy – an artificer I think they called them – and attractive in his uniform. Alec was tall and blond. Both were young and out for a bit of fun. And so was Doris; she was in her element with them both, and with Tom, and the captain. She was sleeping in one of the attic rooms and she had played tricks on each of them. So what should they do but crawl up the stairs where there followed a lot of horseplay.

From my bedroom, I listened to it, half in anger, half in envy. I was young and I would have liked to have joined in the fun, but I was the proprietress. Then there came a loud voice from the landing. Mr Rouyl was demanding I put a stop to this noise. What was this? A house full of hooligans or a nursing home? If I was in charge, why couldn't I keep order? What was I anyway, a guest-house proprietress, or a laundry manageress? I wanted to sort myself out and attend to one business at a time.

Yes, indeed, I wanted to sort myself out and attend to one business at a time. How right he was.

Anyway, there was the garden getting out of hand again – my concrete paths around the house had never been finished. I had laid the rubble, but had never managed to get the coloured blocks onto it, although I had finished the pool and that was very attractive. So I followed Mrs Burgess's advice and got in touch with the authorities, and Harold joined the household. He was in his middle twenties, six foot tall and gangly with a smiling face and a great sense of humour. So why was he classed as mentally deficient? We were to find out. He not only wet the bed, he did his business in it.

This seemed so off, for he could go days and days and remain clean.

I had a talk with him – being used to dealing with the mentally deficient, I had no embarrassment in bringing up the subject. Why did he do it?

He didn't know.

When he felt the urge to go to the lavatory, why didn't he get up?

Oh, because he felt tired.

Would he try to get up in the future?

Oh, yes, yes, Miss Mac, he would, he would.

As for his work, he was all right when he was supervised, but he tended to . . . rest a lot when he wasn't.

Unlike Mrs Burgess's boys, who had to eat in the stable, Harold ate with us at the kitchen table. And I recall the meals were merry. He had a way of telling a story. I realised with sadness that if the little kink in his mind could be erased, here was a first-class comedian.

We were having some work done outside, and as Harold got on well with everybody, he palled up with one of the young men on the job. He wasn't allowed to go out on his own, so this young fellow took him to the pictures and around the town. It was from this association that Harold's personality underwent a change. He talked more: not about amusing things, but about getting a proper day's pay for a proper day's work. This would only slip out now and again, but I knew he was being coached by his new friend and, of course, he was susceptible to suggestion.

Then one day Harold just disappeared. The authorities had to be notified. His new friend said he knew nothing about him, where he might have gone or anything else. I didn't believe him.

They never found Harold, but at Christmas I had a letter written in a big childish scrawl. The envelope was postmarked to indicate it had come from Manchester. The letter said he hoped I was well and he was well, and he wanted to say thank you for me being so nice to him and he would always think of me.

I sat and cried and in a way longed for Harold to come back as if he were a lost child. The following year I had a Christmas card from him; it said, 'Still going strong.' Then the war came and I heard no more. I wonder what became of Harold? Perhaps he married and had a family – some of them might have been slightly mentally defective, but there would be one who would become a leading comedian. Nice thought . . .

So these were some of the men in my life that Smith had referred to.

I had lived in The Hurst for three years with Tom, yet on the day I married him I was a virgin and he too. That was one thing that filled my mind during my week of hate as I look back on that period: how many other people besides Madame Blaut and Nan had painted this picture of the men in my life?

For some long time after that, when people would stare at me, I imagined what they might be thinking. There were definitely at least two people who had been put in the picture, for when Nan and I separated, they severed their allegiance to me when up until then we had been close friends.

This experience is why I take a different view from the general on scandals I read or hear about, for if ever a life has been misjudged, it has been mine – and right from the beginning. Even with regards to Kate, I was verbally attacked and put in the wrong by one of my cousins on a visit to the North. I was staying with my cousin, Sarah, and she gave a party so all the family could meet me instead of me trailing round from one house to the other. I wasn't feeling too good, and there, when everybody was reminiscing and talking about how wonderful their Aunt Kate had been, I was forced to say in front of them all, 'Yes, she would have been a wonderful woman if it hadn't been for the drink.' Michael, a twin cousin, turned on me, saying, 'Don't you dare say a word against me Aunt Kate. You're not fit to wipe her boots,' and more words to that effect. I ask myself now, why didn't I turn on him, on them all, and tell them they hadn't had to live with their wonderful Aunt Kate, and that she had a façade like an iron plate and I was underneath it? No, I remained quiet because I was in Sarah's house, but I recall the great effort it took not to burst out crying. I also recall that when I reached home, I lay in Tom's arms while I told him and asked, 'Why? Why?'

12

Doctors again. I don't know exactly when it was that I transferred to the lady doctor – the one I have already referred to as the convert – or exactly how long I was under her indifferent care. Fifteen years? More like twenty, I should imagine. But like other hurtful things that have happened in my life, her treatment of me remains clear.

During those years, there were times when I was pretty physically ill, but as I've said, once you've had a breakdown, everything that happens to you from then on is associated with it – in my case from primula and ivy poisoning and conjunctivitis to appendicitis, adhesions, womb scrapings, three bouts of pneumonia, phlebitis, suspected cancer of the stomach, anaemia, spinal trouble, gastroenteritis, hiatus hernias et cetera. Yes, all were connected with my breakdown and put down to nerves or imagination.

Tom would never phone her, so I trailed to her surgery even when, at times, I felt I wasn't able to stand because I was so weak from blood loss.

I may appear bitter against this woman, but with due cause. There was the occasion when I was attending hospital for a frozen shoulder. I had written about fifteen books by this time in longhand and the nerves had given out. I thought my writing career was ended. It was Tom who saved it by saying, 'Why not get a tape recorder?' They were enormous in those days with huge reels, but I took to it like a duck to water. However, this particular hot day I was due for a treatment and, as often happens to me when in hospital, something went wrong. It seemed only slight at the time, but instead of being under the lamp or whatever it was for four to ten minutes, the nurse forgot I was there and I had more than double the time.

My cousin Sarah and her husband were staying with me because Tom was at camp, and we all went to the beach. But after an hour, the heat was so intense we had to leave. That evening, they went to the pictures, and as I sat reading in the drawing room I was suddenly overcome with this dreadful feeling. I cannot describe it from this distance, but I know that I was terrified and unable to get to the phone for some time. Eventually, I crawled on my hands and knees into the hall and called the doctor's house, which was in the next road.

'What's the matter now?' she said. What had I been doing to get in this state? When I managed to tell her about lying on the beach and previously being very hot when I came out of hospital, she remarked, 'Oh, you've got sunstroke. I'll be round. Go to bed,' she said. I couldn't – I couldn't get off the floor. I recall she helped me upstairs, then she left a note for my cousin which read, 'Kitty is in bed. She's had a dizzy turn.'

I was in bed for a full week and at times I went a little delirious, but I never saw her again during that time.

I now understand you can die from sunstroke.

With my first bout of pneumonia, she came once. Tom saw me through it. During the second bout three years later, she put in one appearance and ordered drugs that caused such violent diarrhoea, I couldn't keep any food in my body at all and was ill for three months. I only survived at these times with Tom's care. As for my bleeding, she dismissed it as one of those things, so obscure that nothing could be done for it.

My nerves always reached breaking point when I had to visit her surgery, but whereas she had no consideration for me, she did try to do something for Tom's migraine.

She was fond of Tom, but unfortunately her efforts in his direction were of no avail.

I recall the only time she showed concern was when I had phlebitis in both legs. Phlebitis was one thing I was afraid of, as I always look back on it as a lead-up to the breakdown. On this occasion, she ordered that I must rest, but she didn't pay a return visit.

Then there was the period when I was in bed with spinal trouble for months on end. I didn't call her, not once, because as she had said, everyone has backache. On this day, I was dying to get out for a change, so Tom got me into the car – I had difficulty in walking; in fact, I just shuffled. It was a bitterly cold day, the worst time to go out after having been in bed for a long period. On our return, I was shivering and as I stepped up onto the outside porch, a matter of six inches, my legs gave way and I fell flat on my face.

Inside the house, I said to Tom, 'Give me a drink of something – brandy or anything.' He brought me a glass of port and I did what I've never done in my life before, I downed it all in one go to stop my shivering. This was at two o'clock in the afternoon. By three, I was passing blood. When later it was filling the pan, I showed Tom. Immediately, he got on the phone; it had just turned four o'clock. A man's voice answered; he was a kind of caretaker for the doctors who took messages when they were out. He informed Tom that the doctor had been at her clinic, but it was closed now and she was not available for the weekend. Tom demanded to be put through to her. No, he couldn't do that; she was off duty.

I've never seen Tom so angry. He now got on to her home – the private house in the next road. She answered. Oh, very well, she'd come round.

A half hour later, still no sight of her. Tom did something that still amazes me because he had always been so diffident towards her, never wanted me to trouble her and would rather see me crawl to the surgery than phone her. Yet on this occasion he put a coat around me and almost carried me up the drive and into the car and deposited me on her doorstep. She herself opened the door. She was surprised, but so polite. Oh, she was just about to come.

This was on a Friday night. I bled steadily all during the night and part of the Saturday. By then, I was only dimly aware of what was going on. The only thing I knew was the specialist hadn't arrived yet, nor did he arrive on the Sunday or the Monday or the Tuesday. By the Wednesday, I said to Tom, 'Well.' It was a word that expressed all my feelings concerning her treatment of me during the years I'd been under her uncaring care.

When Tom phoned her, she said, 'Oh, oh, hasn't he been there yet?'

What Tom should have answered was, 'No! Nor have you been yet.' The facts are that she hadn't bothered to phone the specialist nor to come. When the specialist – a very nice man who had operated on me the previous year for suspected cancer, but fortunately had found only adhesions – came, he had me taken straightaway to the hospital and into the theatre. His diagnosis was that it could have been a burst telangiectases, as it wasn't cystitis or anything appertaining to that kind of thing.

This incident proved to Tom how right my opinion of her over the years had been, but made him more hesitant than ever of getting in touch with her.

Then I had a third dose of pneumonia.

Previous to this, on going to her surgery while bleeding, she had said I should eat raw pigs' liver and take hogs' blood. How I stuffed these nauseating ingredients down me I don't know, but I caught pneumonia. When I could hardly breathe, Tom phoned her. Her answer to him was that she could do nothing, everybody got colds, keep her warm.

Keep me warm? He was changing me three times a night because the bedsheets were sodden. I'd gone through every nightie I had. At the end of a week, there were nineteen sheets at the laundry. We hadn't any more – only those I was lying in. He went out and bought some and two nighties. I still have them. David Nieper nighties. They were marvellous in those days; I can't say the same for them today. Incidentally, I recall he paid ten pounds for each of them, which nearly caused my demise. Ten pounds for a nightie! I don't know how he got through that time, for he was up most nights, then rushing to school, dashing back at break, then at dinner time to get me to drink and endeavour to get me to eat this raw liver.

The climax came on the Friday night – two o'clock in the morning to be exact. My body seemed to explode and everything in me poured from every vent in it. When I think of the state of that bed and what Tom had to cope with, I don't know how he stuck it. But he wouldn't have left – he still won't – in case he was caught off guard; and this applies to everything.

Sheila White, my neighbour, came in the next morning and as soon as she saw me she ran downstairs and said, 'You know Kitty's dying. You must get some help. Get the doctor at once.'

Tom phoned her.

What was the matter with me?

I had pneumonia and he explained what had happened in the night.

Perhaps it was the expulsion from my body of that hogs' blood and liver – which I've discovered since act as poisons – which saved me.

At three o'clock, she came, sat by the bedside and said, 'Now what's the matter, Kitty?' Her tone indicated I was never off her doorstep. I recall I just lay looking at her. And then she said something I've never been able to forget. 'You know, Kitty,' she said, 'there are old men and women who trail to my surgery when they're feeling like death. They wouldn't dream about phoning me. But of course they've got . . .' She paused and we stared at each other, and then I supplied her words. 'Gumption?' I croaked.

'Yes, that's the word, Kitty. They've got gumption.'

I've always given myself the credit for rising to the occasion. I might be feeling like death, but if something is demanded of me, I'll get through it, even if I collapse after. And that something came to my aid that day. 'How dare you,' I croaked, 'say that I haven't got gumption? It's only by gumption that I've survived all my life. Don't you dare say that to me. Get out!' She got out, went downstairs and said to Tom, 'I think I've upset Kitty.'

Upset me? I cried and cried with the injustice that life seemed to deal me from every quarter and definitely from her over the years.

For a long time at this period, Tom had been suffering martyrdom with his migraine. He had been to see doctors in Hastings, and he had been up to Harley Street, but nothing seemed to touch it. How he went to school and got through his work I'll never know, but sometimes he would return at nights as if he were drunk. I knew a lot of it was due to nerves and stress at school. He was starting to hate the school. He had been made head of the lower school at the time when he should have been made assistant master. It was a piece of chicanery that hurt him, but he would never push himself or say anything. He was beloved of the boys from the second-year intake up to those who were young men waiting to go to university. He helped so many underdogs – ones that other masters dismissed. Two cases in point: Tom took under his wing a doctor's son – who one master had classed as mental – which of course had to be after school and at weekends. The boy passed his exams and was so grateful that he saved up his pocket money for weeks until he could buy Tom a gold wristwatch. Odd, but Tom could never receive gifts graciously. He could give, but he couldn't receive. However, he valued that boy's efforts, as his mother said that they could have given him the money straightaway – they were well off. There was an optician in the town with two boys in school who were both dismissed by masters, and the parents were very worried. They came under 'Cookie's wing', and never did I go into that optician's room over the years, but that man brought the matter up and said his sons wouldn't be where they were today if it hadn't been for Tom. Both achieved success in their different fields.

Again and again, parents would stop me in the street and say what a difference there had been in their boys since they had come under 'Cookie'. He was a real Mr Chips[9] and he became known as that.

Anyway, all he wanted – and all I wanted for him – was to leave the grammar school. Looking back now, I cannot imagine that my aim was to save £5000, because I knew he could retire on that. This was in the late 1960s. How things have changed.

His head became so bad that he knew he would have to give up, and so he took early retirement and lost quite a bit of gratuity, because we agreed if anything should happen to him I would get a pension of eight pounds a week – equivalent to about a £100 these days.

But he had only left the school for about three months when one day there came to the front door three young men with a petition from the sixth form asking if he would come back. I was so touched. And then there were the times, which deeply embarrassed him but made me proud, when we would go to speech day or one of the other events at the school, and on every occasion someone would get up and sing his praises, not just in a few words, but going on and on. Naturally, this caused jealousy, and I recall meeting a master in the middle of town one day – one I knew had always been jealous. He asked how Tom was and I said, 'Oh, doing fine.'

'Give him a message from me,' he said. 'Tell him the school is surviving without him.' There are male bitches as well as female ones.

But now that Tom was clear of the grammar school, it was my turn to be clear of my doctor. I heard of an oldish doctor in St Leonards by the name of Gabb, and I phoned to ask if he would take me as a private patient. The answer was, yes, of course he would.

---

9   The eponymous schoolteacher in the novel *Goodbye, Mr Chips* by James Hilton (published 1934).

I didn't have an occasion to meet this man for some months. I never went to the doctor when I bled. But we had someone staying with us who took ill, so I called him in. It happened that when he arrived, Tom had to see to him because I was having a bleeding. Nothing much compared with my usual dos. But seeing me, he said, 'Do you have many of these?' And when I put him in the picture, he stared at me in silence for some time and he said, 'Nothing's been done? Don't tell me that.' And I said, 'Oh yes, I am telling you that. Nothing can be done.'

'Nonsense,' he said. 'Something can be done about everything, even if it is only alleviation. We'll have to see about this.'

And see about it that man did. Within a fortnight he phoned me: he had been scouting round, he said, and found a man in London by the name of Mr Ranger; he had his place in Harley Street, but he attended Middlesex Hospital. He had spoken to him, and what I was to do was to get in touch and make an appointment.

I couldn't believe it, nor could Tom. My world had turned topsy-turvy. *A doctor* . . . a doctor was showing some actual, real concern for me. It wasn't right.

I was in for more surprises. We went to London, and there I met Mr Ranger, a charming man who surprisingly seemed to know about telangiectasia; but on examining my nose, he said that there was no live tissue left. The only thing he could suggest, especially for the right nostril, was grafting.

I recall sitting looking at him, shaking my head as I said, 'You know, doctor, for years I've wondered why no one suggested grafting. They can give people new faces, new noses, all kinds of things, so why couldn't they graft?'

He didn't say, well, it was a tricky business and it would be a ten to one chance that it would take, especially in the nostril. No, he said nothing like that; he just filled me with hope. And so on my return I phoned my dear Dr Gabb and told him. I was to have the operation in a fortnight's time, and laughingly he said, 'We'll both be going through it together then.' What a spirit that man had. Knowing what I found out later about how that man was feeling, I'm still amazed at how he could care for someone else when he knew what lay before himself. He was to have an operation for cancer about the same time.

Well, there I was, in a private ward in Middlesex Hospital. The ward itself left a lot to be desired, but the nursing was excellent. Tom came up every day and found me on cloud nine because I couldn't believe I was about to receive proper medical attention. Before the operation, Mr Ranger told me he would also cut a piece out of my tongue. This rather disturbed me because although I was bleeding frequently from there too, I was worried in case it would stop me from talking. I recall that he laughed and said, 'I can assure you, Mrs Cookson, you'll go on talking.'

I woke up to find my face a mass of wires and the feeling that my throat had been cut. I can't recall much about the first day or so, except that there was a great bustle in the ward about seven o'clock in the morning after the operation because great men and surgeons such as Mr Ranger – so they were classed, and rightly – were visiting me, and at that hour. This happened two or three times, so whether it was the first time that this operation had been attempted for my particular trouble, at least in the nostril, I don't know; I only know that he was so concerned for the first three days and it was a good feeling.

He had taken three and a half inches of skin from my thigh and sewn it into the nostril. I knew this for a fact when later he had to take the stitches out. That wasn't very pleasant, but the worst thing of all, I found, was the place from where the skin had been taken. It never dawned on me that it wouldn't be where they had put the skin on but where they took it off that would cause the most pain. But once the stitches were out, I sat for hours in a bath trying to ease the Vaseline pad from the raw flesh. It was excruciating, but try as I might there was a part that wouldn't move, and as I understood that I couldn't go home until that came off, I put myself through agony. But to no avail. I said to Mr Ranger that if I could get home I could sit in the bath longer . . . et cetera, et cetera, but he only laughed at me and said, 'Don't worry, it will come off sometime.'

When the nurses touched it, I squirmed. Then one day a very nice nurse – well, she had been up to that point – said, 'Just let me have a look at it.' She looked at it, then her hand came out like lightning and – wham – I hit the ceiling. At least, I felt like I did. 'There now, that wasn't too bad, was it?' She bent over me laughing while the involuntary tears spurted from my eyes, nose and mouth.

Anyway, I went home and had no more bleeding from that side.

I expected to feel discomfort, but when it went on for days and my nostril seemed to swell, I became anxious. When another week passed and I couldn't breathe, I phoned Mr Ranger and he told me to come up. He put a pair of nippers up the nostril and pulled out so much dried blood I couldn't believe it. Then he examined the grafting, after which he looked at me, smiled widely and said, 'It's taken.' I didn't throw my arms around him, although I wanted to, but when we got out into Harley Street, I caught Tom's hand and actually danced down that street. There weren't many people about, but those who were smiled at us.

Wonderful! Wonderful! Wonderful! At least half my trouble was over.

The grafting is still in place. I have a tiny amount of bleeding at odd times from the edge of it, but that is all. I have another nostril, though. Oh yes, I have another nostril, and finger ends, and a tongue, and innards.

To get back to Dr Gabb. When I returned home, I heard that he had gone through an operation about the same time as myself. Then one day, there he was on the doorstep. He seemed to have lost half his weight. He was so pleased for me, but I was concerned for him.

What had been the trouble?

Cancer. He was going back into hospital the next week, and he knew then he was dying.

But his final thoughtfulness for others was yet to come.

Tom got a letter from him, written from his bed in hospital. He had been looking through American medical journals, he said, and there was this new thing out for migraines. He must send away and get it. Two days after Tom received that letter, Dr Gabb was dead.

He had known his case was hopeless from the beginning, yet he could think of me and, in his very last hours, of Tom. We were just two of his patients, new ones at that. I cried for that man; I missed him as I would have done a father. He was the only doctor in my life who had done anything about the concern he was supposed to feel for me. After almost twenty years of no concern from that woman, this man had been like a ministering angel.

I now came under his assistant, and he too was a caring man, but there was only one Dr Gabb.

As if to make up for the closure of my right nostril, the left got going in full spate, as did the top of my left thumb. This became gangrenous when the veins had broken there and some dirt got in while gardening. Poultices and soaking in almost boiling water did no good, so the top had to be cut off. This was done in a surgery with just a local injection. Tom, waiting in the waiting room, said faces around him blanched as I cried out from time to time. After two goes at it, I had to be almost carried out.

And then there was the week of almost interminable bleeding from the left nostril. The kind man – my new doctor – trying to find some way to stop it, had got in touch with an Indian doctor who told him of this new apparatus. It was a rubber bag with a steel pipe going through it. The pipe was inserted into the nostril and then pumped up. Tom held me in bed while the doctor attempted to insert this. The nostril was raw with bleeding and I yelled the place down, but he persisted because the bleeding, he said, had to be stopped. When it was halfway up, he started pumping.

There are different kinds of crucifixions: that was a particular one, I recall. When the thing kept slipping down, he took sticking plaster and put strips across my upper lip to keep it in place. He was no sooner out of the room than I choked on the blood going down my throat and the thing flew out.

At eight o'clock the next morning, I was in an ambulance heading for London to the Middlesex Hospital. There I saw Mr Ranger again, attended by two other specialists. The nostril, he said, was in a bad state. What had happened? When I explained about the rubber tube, he looked at the other two men and said, 'We threw that out of here ten years ago.' My poor doctor in Hastings had believed what the Indian doctor had said – that it was a new find in the medical world. We're all gullible.

Apparently, there was no possibility of a successful grafting being done on the left side. I don't know why – perhaps it was because there were so many of the things at the top of the nostril, or, as I learned later, that the wall between the nostrils was so thin. I find that when I'm bleeding from two sides, only one side can be cauterised because if they did the other side it would burn a hole through.

Anyway, I was back to square one, in that I was bleeding like a pig most days. Moreover, my right leg was so swollen that I could hardly walk on it and my doctor's advice was, 'Rest and keep your legs up.' I know now that they think the worst thing I can do for this swelling is to rest and keep my legs up, or wear slippers. Slippers are the most damaging things I have found for swollen legs. A pair of soft suede lace-up shoes has been a lifesaver in that direction.

I was also suffering with my back on and off. I had been lying in bed for practically six months of the year following weeks of massage and heat treatment, which did nothing for me, when my doctor said,

'Look, I think you'd better have an X-ray.' This was the first time an X-ray had been suggested for my back.

I had the X-ray, then I had a quick visit from my doctor who brought the X-ray plate with him. The words he used were, 'Horrific. I don't know how you've been able to walk about, woman.' Apparently, there were some locked vertebrae at the bottom of the spine. This was likely caused by the fall I'd had in the school yard all those years ago. I'd had to fight, through exercise, to keep myself from leaning to the left – not politically – all my young days. The other parts of the spine, he said, were mush, only kept together by muscles, and these were affected by arthritis. It was a mess of a spine.

Well, well. We were at last finding things out. But Dr Gabb and his partner had come into my life too late, it seemed. How could I help my spine?

Had I tried swimming?

No.

Well, do that.

The result was that we had a swimming pool made, and it used to take poor Tom twenty minutes to get me down those steps and once across the width of the bath.

But I give myself credit for trying, because within a year I did a hundred yards and could do at least a dozen different kinds of strokes, even swimming under water with no hands, so to speak, like the man in the series on television. And I could walk and lift my feet up into the car. I still had pain. I still had to lie on a board – I still do – but I wasn't confined to bed any longer. So the answer to this trouble was to swim.

About this time, there was a great unrest in Tom. He wasn't happy. He seemed to have lost interest in his marvellous garden – the garden that had taken us twenty-two years to make. We had uprooted three sections of woodland, buying a piece at a time, cutting down a mass of old trees and sawing them up. Tom didn't like sawing, so his job was to dig up the great roots, which he did himself – a colossal task. Mine was to de-branch the trees, drag them to the sawing block and saw them up day after day, and, literally, year after year. I loved sawing. I loved seeing a pile of logs, and so even when my back was breaking, I'd be at that sawing cradle using a cross-cut saw alone. Before the period when my back gave out completely, that was my one recreation: spending at least an hour a day sawing then humping the logs indoors to keep the fire going – they saved coal, and for the first fifteen years in Loreto we had no central heating. When we later put in three night storage heaters, we considered them an extravagant luxury – except for the years of evacuation, we had shivered in those two houses nine months of each year.

Tom always said that if he ever had to have help in the garden, he would leave. I've always considered it a fault in him that he never wanted to have help inside or outside the house. But he was still having severe headaches, and they always seemed to be accentuated after a bout of digging – and digging our soil was no light matter, for most of it was dead clay. It was amazing that although the wood had been standing for hundreds of years, there was hardly an inch of topsoil on it: beneath was grey, dead matter as hard as shale to get through.

We had been privileged to have a marvellous builder for four years. He was a two-man business – himself and a labourer – but Mr Russell was a perfectionist when it came to doing work of all kinds. He built us an extension and a garage, and did many things for us in the house. Well. He happened to have a neighbour, and this man was looking for Saturday morning work for his son . . . Could he help in the garden? I was all for it. For years, I had done all the grass-cutting whenever I was able to, and every lawn was on a steep slope. Yet I prided myself I could get round the whole lot in two hours. Some men, I found later, could hardly get round it in two days. But, anyway, the boy was taken on, and then his father joined him just for those few hours on a Saturday morning, but that seemed to finish Tom. From then on, weekends always spelled an awful migraine for him, together with short temper.

Then there was our neighbour. If ever there was a nosy parker she was one, and she had her nose parked into so many lives in the road that she had become feared in a way. Houses were springing up all around us. Although we were on the edge of the wood and had almost three acres of land around the house now so it was private, night time showed how the town had encroached on us, for there were lights all around. Where at one time, there had been half a dozen big houses in the long country road, now there were houses on both sides. This got on Tom's nerves too. But I think the final straw was the episode of the wedding.

In the next road lived a leading figure in the town. He had the same interests as Tom in that he loved rhododendrons and grew them in profusion on his large piece of land. He had, over the years, sold us the thinnings of his shrubs. The first time he visited our garden, he was amazed at the order and the things we had done – such as making a pool from a tiny tricklet of water. This gave him the idea of doing the same thing – only on a bigger scale – from a natural rivulet he had going through the ground.

Over the years, we had become friends [with this man and his wife] in a sort of way. She, because she was a little snob and a name-dropper and – although it still seems ridiculous to me – my name was one that could be dropped. They had a son and a daughter, and from when they were small children I saw to it – like I did to all the other children round about – that they got pocket money. Some of the children had boxes in which I would put sixpence every week towards their spending money at Christmas. An amusing thing happened with regard to their boxes. My close neighbour had two sons and a daughter: the younger son was known as Pos – because of his positive attitude from a baby when he cried for the first two years. We always liked Pos. On a Saturday morning, he would bring his little sister down and there I would put the sixpences in their boxes. This particular Saturday morning he hadn't been down for the previous fortnight, and when I put the sixpence in the box he looked up at me and said, 'You owe me two more.'

'What?'

'You owe me two more sixpences. I haven't been for the last fortnight.'

'Pos,' I said, 'no visit, no sixpence.'

He looked up at me, 'No?'

'No.'

'Oh well, come on.' He grabbed his sister's hand and away they went up the drive. He was five at the time. He's married now and divorced. He wrote to us last Christmas – he sounded sad and somewhat lost. Apparently, he has cut off from home for he said, 'I will likely spend Christmas with some friend or other.' We were always very fond of Pos.

But to get back to our other neighbour. She always said we were the only people who gave her children anything when they were little. I'll say that much for her – she was grateful. But they grew, as children do, and the day of her daughter's wedding came.

She had phoned me earlier saying, 'You'll come, won't you?' I refused invitations from all round and had a reputation for being a very private person, but I said, 'Yes, of course we will come.'

'Put on your best bib and tucker.'

'Of course,' I said. 'I always do.'

The morning of the wedding came and the sun was shining, which was as well, as they were having the reception in the garden – the house was very small. We both felt very unwell that morning. Tom, who had been taking up to twenty tablets – yes, twenty tablets! – a day of aspirin and other things to alleviate the migraine, had suffered a collapse a month previously. This had really been caused by the poison in his body and he had been in bed for a week and delirious for part of the time. I had no one to help and wouldn't call in my neighbour. But things became so desperate, I had to phone my cousin Sarah in Birtley, and she and her husband came straightaway and took over the house while I saw to Tom. The result was that he now had to go for tests on the Monday because his waterworks had become very affected. As for me, I'd had two heavy bleedings that week and also a severe bout of very, very painful indigestion. I didn't know then that its real name was hiatus hernia. So neither of us was feeling fit to attend the wedding, but there we were – me in a green silk two-piece wearing a large brown leghorn picture hat, and Tom in a new suit he had bought the previous week. He looked very dapper. But when we arrived at the church and were met by a hoard of grey-morning-suited young men, there was a question in both our minds. As the church filled up, there were so many black-tailed morning suits present, it looked as if we were attending a funeral instead of a wedding – though I was relieved to see that there were a number of lounge suits here and there.

At the reception, I was introduced to this one and that one as Catherine Cookson, not Mr and Mrs Cookson. I knew very few of the people present, and they stood around and sat around drinking in cliques, but I did notice the scarcity of any near neighbours at the reception, also the attitude of the bride's mother, which was cool. But I put this down to her worrying over the wedding. I knew the bride was going on her honeymoon to an island and, when talking to her, I said, 'Are you leaving today?' and she answered, 'No, we won't be going until tomorrow.' Or indicated as much. She made me think they were staying at this house that night, which I felt was slightly odd, but it passed from my mind in the hubbub.

I think the wedding had been at eleven. When three o'clock came and all the speeches had been made and we had wandered round the garden, Tom said, 'Can we slip away?' I saw that he looked grey and I knew he felt ill. I said, 'I'd better tell her.' And at this I went into the house. Their sitting room was full of people, as was the hall, and she was standing at the door leading into the garden talking to some guests; the marquee was right opposite and people were milling about. I spoke her name and she turned towards me and I said quietly, 'Would you mind if we went now, dear? It's been a beautiful wedding.' I got no further, for she silenced all about her by crying, 'How dare you leave before the bride and bridegroom. Have you no manners? Don't you know the right thing to do?' or words to that effect.

In the hushed silence, I stared at her; her face was contorted with temper. I turned slowly about and walked out without saying a word.

Tom saw that something had happened. He said immediately, 'It's because I didn't turn up in a dress suit.' And I knew he was right. I'd known it all along from the moment we'd come out of church and we'd come face to face with her.

We were both upset and angry. She was considered a little upstart in most quarters. Apparently, she had been brought up by an aunt, but I had met her mother and a sister – I think she had two sisters, but the one I met was a charming woman. As for her mother, I'd met her while she was on holiday at her daughter's and she was a dear, dear soul, but a very ordinary, working-class woman. She lived in the Midlands and had been kept in the background.

On the Sunday, I sat down and wrote her a letter explaining why we had to leave, because Tom and I were ill and didn't want to spoil the wedding if we had collapsed.

That was the end of our association. From then on, the husband would pass Tom in the car without looking at him, whereas before he always stopped and had a chat and was only too pleased to talk gardens.

A friend of hers told me later that there was an excuse for her attitude, for she had been in a state of high nerves for weeks before the wedding. But that, to my mind, was no excuse for insulting me simply because Tom had not turned up in tails – being of small stature, he considered he looked ridiculous in tails and would never wear them.

This incident seemed to be the final straw. Tom wanted to get away. There we were, in this lovely house set in this beautiful garden with a magnificent indoor swimming pool, and he wanted to up and leave it.

At that time, I was becoming greatly in demand to give talks in the North, and we would stay at my cousin's. The outcome of this was we thought, why not take a house and furnish it, and go back to the North for a month at a time? It would give us a break. And this is what we did. We bought a house in Eslington Terrace in the centre of Newcastle, and in 1975 we commuted five times. It was a long journey. I recall the first night we slept in our new abode: I got such a feeling of homesickness for Loreto and Hastings that I cried my eyes out. It seemed utterly stupid, and although Tom kept reiterating that we were going back, it didn't seem to make any difference; I felt I had lost Loreto and the garden. It was a premonition I had, for the more times we came North, the more times Tom didn't want to return to Hastings. So, finally, we decided to move. But there was the question of selling the house.

In 1954 we had paid £3,300 for it. That was a lot of money in those days. In fact, it was so much that the house had stood empty for a time before we bought it, and the nurse to whom it had been left by the owner was getting a bit desperate. It stood in half an acre of ground and, apart from the house, the grounds were on a slope: the drive was so steep it was impossible to get a car up it – down yes, but never up. We worked on the inside of the house for years. We eventually built on a twenty-foot room and kitchen. We took three pieces of land at one side, and in the twenty-two years that followed we transformed them into beautiful gardens. They were so fine that people came from miles to see them.

The house, being situated on a hillside, had no garage. But when we first took it, there was a strip of land and a huge garage big enough to hold a couple of boats for sale right next door. The lot was up for £250. We were asked if we would like it. Well, we hadn't a car and never even thought of having one because we couldn't afford it – why, a car would cost £300 or more, and we were both terrified of debt. So, to my everlasting regret, I let that piece of land and the garage go. But when I was told I might have relief in my back if I swam, we decided to have a pool built. But where? The man next door was talking of selling that strip of land and the garage. How much for? Eight thousand pounds.

Where in 1954 we couldn't afford £250, we could now buy that piece of land – a narrow strip not more than 60 feet wide and 210 feet long – at the exorbitant and brazen price of £8,000.

From the previous owner of the next-door house we had bought a little garage leading out onto the other road and a narrow right of way through the bottom of his garden. So altogether we had made five additions of land to the house. Then we had a big garage built at the top of the steep drive. And these were only the main things, not taking into account the thousands of pounds spent on the garden, the new bathroom et cetera. My books told me – not counting our labour of twenty-two years, nor the cost of the thousands of azalea plants and hundreds of rhododendrons and other specimens, and the £16,000 for the pool – that we had spent close on £50,000. So, as property was, in those days, we thought it was only fair to ask £70,000. Someone suggested we would get £90,000 because this swimming pool was really a beautiful affair that led direct from the study and had a huge patio outside with gardens falling away. But no, we said, we would be very happy with £70,000. When a local agent came and offered us £45,000 for it, I felt like throwing him out of the door for his nerve. His reason for his price was that Hastings was going down the hill. If I was nearer London, then I could have asked £150,000, and likely got it.

By this time, Sarah and Jack had been looking round at houses in the North for a permanent place for us, and were very enthusiastic about a renovated church. So we hied through and saw the church: it was very nice indeed, but not half as big as Loreto, and it would mean getting rid of most of our furniture. But it was out in the country next to a farm near Morpeth, so we decided to take it. But there was still our house to deal with.

When we did get an offer near what we wanted, it was on the condition that the most beautiful part of the garden could be sold as building plots. The thought of all those years of work and that beautiful stretch of shrubs being ripped up for a building plot nearly made us decide to stay.

Then I thought of Foster Barker, the husband of my cousin's daughter. He had always loved the house right from the first time he saw it, but could never hope to aspire to anything like it. I had given him a helping hand over the years, and he had pleased me by putting me in touch with pieces of furniture for sale through a small London paper he took. So I got on the phone with him and said, 'Foster, how would you like to have Loreto?' I understand now he nearly collapsed. He had worked for ICI [Imperial Chemical Industries], but was now running a café, and a place like Loreto was way out of his reach. However, I made it possible for him to have it at £55,000. He could pay the same amount he was paying to the building society for his own house each month, and use the money from the sale of his house as a deposit, and the rest would be paid in six years when he would sell his business to clear the debt. Fortunately for him, he gave up the café and took a fish and chip shop and he did so well he could have cleared the debt off within three years – so much for fish and chip shops.

It was a terrible wrench for me to leave that place, especially the garden. But fortunately, his wife Rosemary loved the garden and I knew she would look after it, which she has done. And as for Foster, he says to this day he cannot believe his luck.

Well, we might not have made anything from those years of work in that place, but it is satisfying to both Tom and me that it's still being cared for.

But we didn't leave Loreto to go to the little church. It had become a necessity for me to swim, so we wanted to build a pool. We asked the man from whom we were buying the house, a Mr Moss, whether he knew anyone who built pools. He said he would look around. Well, we stayed in the North a fortnight and needed to get back to Hastings. I had frequently phoned Mr Moss to ask if he had found anyone yet, and this particular morning he asked if we had signed the deeds. I told him we had, and that they had gone off that morning. 'All right,' he said. 'I'll pick you up and take you to a man who builds pools.'

He took us to Town Barns, a beautiful house with a gallery, and through the drawing room we could see a magnificent pool. Mr John Anderson was the man who built pools. When I asked him how much a pool like that would cost to make, he said about £27,000. Then he asked if I had bought the church. When I said yes, he said, 'What a pity – this is up for sale.'

I could, at that point, have phoned my solicitor and withheld the deed because I knew that this man Moss had known all along who could build pools, but he'd wanted to clinch his deal first, knowing that when we saw this house we would buy it. It had everything that we wanted at that moment. John Anderson said immediately, 'If you want to buy this, I'll do a deal with you for the church.'

So that is what happened. But Mr Moss was hardly out of his house when he phoned John Anderson and said, 'She'll want to buy your place, so stick another ten thousand on – she's got it.' I've never met that man since. I hope I never shall.

John Anderson was a developer and he was in a tight corner, and although we knew very little about him we helped him out.

So, in the short time we had been in Newcastle, we had bought three houses: 39 Eslington Terrace, The Church and Town Barns . . .

It was a beautiful morning when Foster, Rosemary and the family arrived to take over. I felt heartbroken. I didn't know what Tom really felt, only that he was glad to leave Hastings. But Foster and Rosemary were ecstatic with happiness, which was something.

Two huge vans with loads of furniture had gone on ahead the previous day. It was a colossal task getting settled into the new house. The only thing that marred it was that we looked out onto a stone wall; beyond that there was a courtyard where there were another three houses – one, a large new building as big as our own and the other, a row of cottages occupied by a farm worker and a lady who had lived there for many years.

Tom still insists that one of the main reasons he wanted to move was to get me nearer my own folk in case anything happened to him, because I kept so aloof in Hastings and had few real friends, if any. Strong acquaintances, yes, but friends are a different thing altogether. So we started our life in the North, and it would provide me with such medical care as I'd never had – except from my dear Dr Gabb in the short time we knew each other – and that alone satisfied Tom and gave him justification for our move.

Those first months in Town Barns were memorable in that, although I loved the pool and the house at first, I cried every night for Loreto and that garden.

Then there were the people of the village – or the small town, which Corbridge has now become. The first head-on clash with them came when we bought the dirty thistle- and weed-strewn field that bordered the road and part of our garden. We understood that it was going to be sold as building land, and the old lady who lived at the bottom of the lane had approached us to see if we could do anything about it because her cottage looked straight onto the field. Well, we did something about it: for £27,500 we bought that field with the intention of turning it into a garden. This brought a spate of fanatics at us. The field was supposedly an ancient glacier and should not be dug. We didn't know then that the corporation had laid drains across it four feet deep. Then came anonymous letters, so we decided to leave and made this known in the local paper and why.

This paper came out on a Friday morning. By eight o'clock, there was a stream of people at the door and it went on all weekend. They didn't want us to leave the village just because of one or two cranks. But one of our visitors protested strongly about my elusiveness. The people of the village wanted to see me more: why didn't I walk through the village more? Why didn't I show myself more? I said I was in very poor health and, anyway, I was always busy. That didn't seem to matter; I should still mix.

If anything kept me from walking in the village, this lady's attitude did.

In the next two years, it cost us well over £20,000 to have this huge field landscaped and tree-bordered and 20,000 daffodils planted, besides 10,000 crocuses and other specimen trees. People came from different parts to admire the garden and told us so, but there were still others against it, and over the years their snide remarks became unbearable to Tom and myself.

But that wasn't the worst experience at Town Barns. What almost did make us fly the place was the report in the Newcastle *Journal* following my talk at the opening of a medical week aimed at bringing people's attention to their medicine cabinets and encouraging them to get rid of old pills and medicine bottles. Strangely, from the moment I was asked to carry out this function, I had an odd feeling about it. The day before the event, I said to Tom, 'I don't want to go to this thing in Morpeth. It's difficult to know what to say. How about this?' And so I went over the short speech I was going to make.

After living with a man for near on forty years, as it was then, it is difficult to make him laugh, but Tom thought this speech very witty and his response told me that this was the right thing to say. However, imagine my horror and amazement when the paper heading was, 'Catherine Cookson says everybody should be made to pay for their medicines and medical attention. She said she's proud of being a private patient.'

It took up the front page, and everything I had said that was supposed to be humorous was twisted. The Labour councillors who had been present went for me, and said I must be mad saying that a lot of people went to the doctor's surgery out of habit or because they just wanted to talk. Yes, I had said that, and it was right, and all the doctors there shook my hand and congratulated me on the talk after. So the attack came as a double surprise.

Well, this is the end, we thought. We could stand no more. Again we had people saying, 'Don't take any notice,' 'Please don't go,' and telling us that someone needed to speak out like that about the National Health . . . I hadn't spoken against the National Health, but the report made out that I thought all old people should be made to pay for their treatment.

A side effect of this business was that I didn't go out of the house – even into the garden – for weeks, and I couldn't pass the row of old people's houses near us, even months later, without feeling that the old people were saying, 'There she goes, bragging about being able to afford private medicine.'

Then came the morning when I was all dressed up to go to the television studios in Newcastle to do ten epilogues. I was leaving the bedroom when the phone rang. It was a male voice on the other end, one I hadn't heard before, and I couldn't understand what he was saying. So he said, 'Will I explain it to you?' I said, 'Please do.' And he did just that. I was appalled at the filth I was listening to, and finally I cried, 'I'll get the police.' It was an obscene phone call, the first I'd had, and it shook me, but at the same time it made me realise that part of me was still very innocent. The police inspector said he was terribly sorry about it, but they got literally dozens of calls every day with the same complaint.

There was another house – Trinity – similar to ours and quite close, that had been built at the same time. We were in Town Barns a year before I spoke to the owner. Then a short while after that, the house went up for sale, but it didn't sell. One morning, my neighbour came in for something and she became tearful, telling me that she couldn't stand the house, she had never liked it since they had moved into it. She had been used to a rambling old place with plenty of outhouses where she could store junk – she was interested in repairing chairs and was a frequent attender of auction salerooms.

At this time, we were having quite a lot of visits from business associates and Tom was always cooking, so we got the idea of helping to relieve Margaret's distaste for her home by using it as an annex for whoever wanted to come and look after themselves. Moreover, as there was only a long dividing wall between us, it would open up the garden and provide us with a big lawn.

The owner had had way-out ideas in his planning and had put in a huge stone staircase that would have been better suited to a medieval hall than a space the size of an ordinary room. So the first thing we did was to have the hall gutted. It seemed a sacrilege to tear the inside of a new house to bits, but we also took away a bedroom, above which extended the gallery, and replaced all the narrow glass doors with wider ones, and I was in my element in decorating and furnishing the house. The finished article was a thing of beauty. It was better altogether than Town Barns, and greatly admired. It had two natural stone arches – one leading to the kitchen and one from the hall into the dining room, which at one time had led into the cowsheds, for the whole place had been an old farm.

When we bought this house from the owner, we also bought their cottage, Hill House, up in the hills, which had a spectacular thirty-foot room. We took it to give us a break and get away from the constant pestering and interruptions in Town Barns – for I had become a focal point for tourists and there would be buses stopping on the road outside, people picnicking beside the side gate and men walking the walls with cameras. Someone had put me on the sightseeing list on the holiday touring buses doing circular tours from Durham.

So there we were with three houses: we had bought five since coming to the North three years previously, but had only really lived in one. Three lots of rates, water rates, telephone, electric, repairs, alterations and what have you – on and on.

I think we reached moving point when we had a break-in to Trinity. Five local youths pushed one of their gang horizontally through a small pane of glass about twelve by nine. They were disturbed, but they got off with a magnificent pair of church candelabra, a small antique table and various other things. The silver they had arranged in the middle of the room ready to pick up.

This was a bitter pill for Tom to swallow, for he had helped various sporting events in the village.

One day when we were passing the very kiosk where I had stopped and phoned my cousin after what to me was a disastrous journey over Alston, Tom stopped, and pointing to a side road, said, 'Let's go up and see that lake that Mr Cowell was talking about with the house for sale about it.' Mr Cowell was our painter. I recall I protested strongly. I wasn't feeling well and I knew we'd have to drive by the side of a ravine. However, up that road we went and there was the lake. It looked lovely, and Tom said, 'Would you like to go and look at the house because we must find someplace to give us a break away from Corbridge.' I thought, 'He's right.' So once back home, I phoned Mr Robb, the owner of the furniture store in Hexham who also owned the house, and asked if we could view it.

By the way, we had passed over our cottage to my cousin's son in order that he could get married.

The next morning at half past ten, I stepped out of the car at the top of a curved drive and looked on a covered way that was cluttered with logs and oddments of one thing and another, including a wheelchair. But as soon as I stepped into that front door, across the small hall and into the sitting room and looked out onto the lake from one of the windows, I said immediately, 'I'll take it.'

That's the most foolish thing to do when viewing a house. I'd had experience in buying houses, so why did I jump in like that? The sitting room was thirty feet long, as was the dining room, and there was a large kitchen with rooms and a large utility room off it. There was also a row of cottages comprising three bedrooms – they were 300 years old and smelt of age, but that didn't deter me. What almost did was the sight of the swimming pool at the other end of the bungalow. It was the dirtiest place I'd ever come across. The windows were rusted and two rusty poles across the corner held plastic sheeting and served as dressing rooms. The boiler house was in a little wooden erection with a leaking roof, so all the expensive equipment had rusted. I later learned it was where the previous owner had kept her goat.

Outside at the end of the cottages was a pile of stones that had once been the wash house, and further on a dilapidated building that had served as a blacksmith's shop many years ago. Two of its walls were being held up for half its length by a bank of ashes, residue from the cottage over many years. And, of course, I wasn't seeing it through Tom's eyes; he had already noticed the shoddy brickwork on the outside. Running his fingers along the pointing, it came away like sand.

Still, it was out in the wilds, it had a most magnificent view and there was the lake lying a few yards from the doorstep.

It had been advertised for £105,000, but the sight of us, and knowing who we were, caused the lady to explain that it had been withdrawn from the market on the advice of an agent as being undervalued; it was now priced at £115,000. It was robbery. We knew we were buying the view – without that view they would have been lucky to get £70,000 . . . I forgot to mention the conservatory that joined the sitting room to the swimming pool. The brickwork supporting the flower beds and the tiled floor were smeared all over with cement – it took Tom days on his hands and knees applying a strong acid to get that floor clean, and that was only the beginning.

When the lady asked for £10,000 extra for the carpets, some curtains and fittings, I realised we were being robbed, but we went on. After putting the money down in cash almost immediately to help them buy another place, we let them stay in the house for six weeks rent free. But on the day they were leaving and we were moving in, she made another bid. Not satisfied with what she had got out of us, she asked would we like to have the bookcase in the kitchen? It was a modern affair that you buy in sections, and had a table and four chairs to match . . . 'Well, yes, all right,' I said. 'How much do you want for it?'

'Two thousand seven hundred and fifty pounds.'

Talk about being robbed – that was daylight robbery, especially seeing that they had this huge shop, and naturally all the things they got from it would be cost price or less.

I understood also that Mr Robb was almost in tears having to leave the place, as he had an amphibious machine that he could take onto the lake and also traverse the woods in; now he was moving at his wife's behest into the heart of town because she thought it was too far out for Hexham – it being all of a seven-mile run.

I forgot to say that we had, in the meantime, decided to make this place our living quarters and so move out of Corbridge. We had spent £127,000 so far and we didn't realise we would have to spend that much again within the next three years to get the place to our requirements.

That wouldn't have been so bad, but from the beginning we found so much botched work. Apparently, a lot of the previous owner's altera-tions had been done by joiners from the shop: men used to knocking up shelves and with no idea, it would seem, of real carpentry.

The first thing we decided to do was to get rid of that awful swim-ming pool, have it filled in and make it into a drawing room in order to take the furniture I had collected over the years and which I hated to part with. After a lot of delays, we got permission to do just that, with the addition of a bedroom and bathroom above. It turned out to be a splendid addition, but in the end the bills touched on £80,000.

We had only been in the house a week when the wood stove boiler leaked, then the rain poured in through a flat roof, and we were trou-bled by a strong musty smell coming from the cottages.

Again, I forgot to mention that at the other end of the house we had a study built onto another flat roof. One thing we didn't discover until we saw the deeds was that we did not own our drive or the front-age running along between the front and back doors. That belonged to the farmer. So we had to negotiate and buy that. At the further side of the house, where the old bothy stood, was a dump of old bricks and rubbish from the brickyard sheds that covered the space at the back of the house and was used now for housing cattle – so we negotiated for that rubbish dump. Then there was a hundred-foot wall to be built to border our land, fences to go up, at least two centuries of ashes to be moved away from the bothy and that renovated. Then there was the 300 feet of lake bank to be fortified because the lake turned into the North Sea in winter or high wind.

Why did we stay in this place? Because it has great compensations. It is isolated in a way, yet the ordinary people round about are kind and thoughtful. I had made it plain to the so-called gentry, even before I moved in, that our reason for taking this place was for privacy. I didn't add that I didn't intend to waste my time with callers who had nothing better to do than see who this Catherine Cookson really was. My main object in life when we moved here was to get away from people, for the previous five years of my life hadn't been my own. We welcome our friends, but they are few.

It's a strange thing about people who are in the news – they've just got to shake hands with someone and that someone claims them as a lifelong friend. I feel sorry for pop stars and actresses and people with titles, yet some seem to enjoy it. I must be an oddity.

But back to the house. We have been here now three years and our latest find is that the cottages have had to be gutted. We decided to have a small porch put outside the door of the cottage leading into the garden. We knew that the carpet in the middle bedroom was damp, but when the builder examined the floorboards, he found that in the main they were covered with plywood – in order to lay the wall-to-wall carpet, I suppose, that I had bought with the house. Underneath this, the floors were rotten and had actual gaping holes in them, and underneath that were inches of hanging fungi and dry rot. But this wasn't all. The whole cottage had been a community centre for rats and mice; the men found their dead corpses by the dozen and the rodents had eaten the linings out of the partitions and the covering of the pipes to make their nests. No wonder there had been a smell. Not only had all the floors to come up, but the partitions between the rooms were ripped out. It had been understood that the men would take three or four days to make this porch; they have now been here seven weeks and the decorators have just gone in. We reckon there will be another £20,000 bill all told.

When my secretary made a rough estimate last month of what we had spent on the bungalow, it ran to over £250,000. Ironically, we could have had a lovely estate in the South for this. Still, we have the lake and the privacy. But we also have that forty-five-minute run into Hugo's when I have a bleeding, which has been so frequent lately that we did, some weeks ago when I had my seventh emergency run in seventeen days, think we should move again and get nearer Newcastle. But no – I'm finished with moving.

Mentioning Hugo, I must get onto doctors again.

13

One thing had concerned Tom about coming North. Would I be able to find a doctor there? Of course, as he said, there would be dozens of them, but would there be one who could understand my trouble? I was thinking along the same lines, but from when we moved into Town Barns in the September of 1976, I wasn't in need of a doctor until the Christmas of that year. Although still homesick for Loreto – not Hastings – I was fully occupied during the day. I bled now and again, but nothing that I called heavy until around Christmas time, when the local man had to be called in. He was short – the same size as Tom – young, definitely a northerner, and very nice.

'Oh, something should be done about this. I'll get you to Mr Harle in Newcastle and he'll give you a thorough overhaul.'

No frowning here against the suggestion of a second opinion. In fact, it wasn't even thought about on my part, and I knew this new fellow would have all my records from Hastings . . . She'd had a breakdown, this, that and the other. But there was no suggestion in his manner of, 'My God! Another one of them. What hasn't she had? Most of it thought up from the breakdown likely.' No, not with this fellow. 'I'll be in tomorrow again,' he said. And he was.

That was eight years ago, and David Harle has proved himself not only to be a good, caring doctor who is not afraid to admit that something is beyond his knowledge, but has become our very close friend and tells us off for not phoning him in the middle of the night when I need him. Once Tom had to do this when I had become very ill with gastroenteritis, and he put me to sleep then sat with me for an hour. As he jokingly said later, he thought I was going to pop off and he wanted to be there to see that I went properly equipped for my journey.

When I had a severe pain in my stomach that I'd kept dark for some time, fearing the worst, he brought in another doctor immediately. The result was I was whipped into hospital and the worst didn't happen – it was diverticulitis. But best of all, through him I made the acquaintance of Mr Hugo Marshall, the ear, nose and throat specialist, and here I have discovered another caring man. So caring that Tom just has to ring up at any time of the night or day and I can be whipped to his home. Sometimes he is in the theatre when I get to the RVI [Royal Victoria Infirmary], and he'll come out between jobs and see to me in a side ward.

I hate to have to call either of them in the middle of the night, and even in the daytime we never trouble them unless it's absolutely necessary. David goes for me and says, 'Why didn't you ring me?'

Can you imagine what such treatment means to me, and to Tom, after those long years of neglect? And let me say here, it isn't because I'm Catherine Cookson, for I know that David, who is now head of the group practice, tells his subordinates that they must answer all night calls. Eight times out of ten it might be simple panic on the patient's side, but for the other two it could mean life or death.

He has very few private patients. I think he can count them on one hand. So it isn't for money or prestige he made this rule, but out of humanitarian feelings. Especially for patients who have absolutely been made immobile, unable to move hand or foot with this dreadful thing. David is very heartening altogether. Every Monday, he comes for an hour and we have a long chinwag, talking about everything under the sun but illness; we argue, not at all like doctor and patient, but often like two self-opinionated Geordies. And often when he's leaving, I'll say, 'You feel better now?' And laughingly he admits that he does. As Tom says, he can relax here over a cup of tea. A few weeks after we had both talked ourselves dry, I walked with him to the door, and said, 'There's a matter I think we should have cleared up. It's just this: are you going to pay me for your visits by cheque or cash?'

'You,' he said, and went out laughing.

So, I'm fortunate, at last, thank God. I'm fortunate with doctors.

Hugo is a different character altogether. He's almost twice the size of David and has no small talk or chit-chat, but appreciates humour and he is gentle, kind and thoughtful. We have come to know him and Ann closely, and whatever dos we hold here – I must come to them – they're always happy to attend. The last one was a short time ago when we had a dinner party for twelve . . .

We certainly have had some lovely dos since we came here, though I've been in bed with a bleeding or one thing or another almost up to the day before nearly all of them.

It was about this time I learned that I was going to be given a MA by the University of Newcastle. I was delighted, naturally, but Tom was more so – he was overjoyed. It's amazing how he can be so happy for me. As I've said, what a change of attitude. And I thank God for it, as things have been hitting me from all sides over the past few years.

My blood count having gone down to sixty-two in 1982, I had a blood transfusion. Funny about that, it seemed to alter my personality and way of thinking for two or three days. I thought it might be my imagination running riot but no, I had a decidedly weird feeling. I wasn't me as I knew me to be. And then towards the end of 1982, the blood count became low again and I was so tired I literally had to drag myself about. I had been dragging myself about for years, of course, but this got so bad that I didn't want to get out of bed – every movement was an effort.

As for getting up into the study and tackling that mail, looking back I wonder how I managed it day after day, although I knew part of this feeling was caused through neurasthenia. Oh yes, I've got that too. I wouldn't face up to it for years. I used to call it exhaustion, but after the breakdown I had these weird bouts of energy and depression, during which I could lose the power of speech and movement. And the only way to bring myself out of it was to turn on myself, so to speak, saying, 'Come on, out of it. No more of it. Get up. You're all right.' I'd had nervous hysteria before the breakdown, but this wasn't like nervous hysteria – there was no quick beating of the heart, no gasping for breath, no feeling of intense excitement or even fear, just an awful feeling of fading away.

David is very heartening. He tells me I'm my own best doctor. I really don't need him, because I manage the neurasthenia the right way and in the only way possible to work myself out of it. He knows.

At this point, the manuscript ends. Catherine died on 11 June 1998, at the age of ninety-one. Tom passed away less than three weeks later, on 28 June.

The notes below were found in Catherine's bedside drawer after she died.

◆　◆　◆

Years ago, young men sang, 'I'm twenty-one today – I'm twenty-one today. I've got the key of the door, never been twenty-one before.'

But today, darling, you are eighty-two. And at twenty-four, you took the key of my heart and you have it still. And you have oiled it with patience, kindness and love, such as is rarely shown.

Fame came to me; I was made a Dame. But the greatest honour was to have your name those long years ago when I had no name of my own.

For fifty-four years, we have weathered the storms, our thoughts really of one accord. Yet nowhere along the road have you sought reward for yourself.

Sunday, 21 August

Darling, it's some weeks since I wrote the above and I can't read a word I said. But now I can say what I'm sure I've said before: that I not only love you but am so grateful to you for your continued care of me, and how you're there for me.

I'm so free with words and I want to tell you this so often, but as you know, every time I do, I cry. And you clasp me in case I bleed. But now I say again, I'm so heartfelt grateful for all you do for me in all ways.

We've had a lovely day today outside all the time and I did the steps up to the garden – that pleased you in spite of you having that awful feeling of anxiety on you.

Oh, dear me, I'm writing quite slowly now – you just brought the coffee in, dear.

Darling – a peaceful birthday

a pain-free birthday

and a birthday full of love from me.

Ever your Kitty.

ABOUT THE AUTHOR

Catherine Cookson was born in East Jarrow near the mouth of the River Tyne, one of the poorest areas in Britain. Her childhood was deeply scarred by violence, fear, alcoholism, shame and guilt, and her books were inspired by her upbringing. She fought hard for a better life and was determined to be a writer. Her readership quickly spread throughout the world, and her many bestselling novels established her as one of the most popular of contemporary women novelists. After receiving an OBE in 1985, Catherine Cookson was made a Dame Commander of the Order of the British Empire in 1993, and was appointed an Honorary Fellow of St Hilda's College, Oxford, in 1997. She died shortly before her ninety-second birthday, in June 1998. By the time of her death, she had written over one hundred books and was the UK's most widely read novelist, and remained the most-borrowed author in UK public libraries for twenty years.

The Cookson Estate recently discovered two unpublished manuscripts – a memoir and a novel – in the attic of Cookson's home. Amazon Publishing will be releasing these two unseen works and the author's backlist will be available through Kindle Direct Publishing, ensuring Catherine Cookson's legacy is available to readers across the globe.